Adeline Dutton Train WHitney

A Golden Gossip

Neighborhood Story NO. II

Adeline Dutton Train WHitney

A Golden Gossip
Neighborhood Story NO. II

ISBN/EAN: 9783744704939

Printed in Europe, USA, Canada, Australia, Japan

Cover: Foto ©Thomas Meinert / pixelio.de

More available books at **www.hansebooks.com**

A GOLDEN GOSSIP

NEIGHBORHOOD STORY NUMBER TWO

BY

MRS. A. D. T. WHITNEY

AUTHOR OF "FAITH GARTNEY'S GIRLHOOD," "THE GAYWORTHYS,"
THE "REAL FOLKS" SERIES, "ODD, OR EVEN,"
"ASCUTNEY STREET," ETC.

BOSTON AND NEW YORK
HOUGHTON, MIFFLIN AND COMPANY
The Riverside Press, Cambridge
1892

CONTENTS.

A GOLDEN GOSSIP.

CHAPTER I.

WILD CLOVER.

MR. EPHRAIM CROOKE built his house in the crook of the road.

His farm lay both ways, at right angles. One line of the country street runs straight down to the Point, where the little Wewachet meets the Shepaug, and they broaden down together toward the sea, — where the last creep of the tide comes up and there is a touch of salt in the water; where the coal and lumber barges moor at the wharf; and behind are the bridge and the old village, with the street of shops, and the railway station and the town hall. In the other direction from Crooke Corner, the highway takes its southern bend, then winds and sheers off again toward the meeting-houses and the Centre, and beyond that to the hills and pasture sides of Shepaug.

The Crooke house, in its two portions, was faced

upon these lines; its front windows looked along both of them. In a sense, they squinted. In this way the inmates got a squint, so to speak, at almost everything that moved about, and it was an invitation to the passers-by, both up and down, so that the Crooke women-folk caught as in a weir all that floated of news or events; it all came in with the frequent callers who made this a half-way stop between the Point village and the " up-street " neighborhoods.

" You always get it, good or bad," cousin Elizabeth said once, with a touch of meaning that her hearers, not quite comprehending, were instantly suspicious of.

She was there on a visit, and a knot of droppers-in had just gone, leaving a lot of conversational drift stuff to be sorted over in after-discussion with the kind of ruminant felicity a certain class of animals is privileged to enjoy.

" It's a right-down gossip corner," Miss Elizabeth had added, good-humoredly enough; but the very good-humor pointed a rebuke with its gentleness.

" Well, why should n't things gether in a corner?" demanded Miss Sarah Crooke. " The snow drifts up here, and the dead leaves, when the wind blows. Why should n't the news? We ain't to blame."

" Why shouldn't you rake out and shovel up a little ? "

" 'Cause we ain't set here on a selery to do the job," shrilled old Ephraim from the stove side, with his pipe in his mouth.

Old Ephraim was not much of a chatterbox himself, but he had certain mechanical, habitual ways of setting the chatter going and keeping it up around him. They all knew he liked it and expected it. It chirped him up, his wife said.

Old Mrs. Crooke knitted round after round on a gray stocking, without opening her lips. She did not hear it all, and besides, she " hated differin' an' contradickshin." For that reason, and because of the entertainment of the other two, the gossips had their own way in her sitting - room, saying this and that of everybody, even when old lady Crooke did hear and knew better. " Father wanted to find out what was going. He hadn't much to think of, and Sarah liked company. She couldn't get out herself ; things had to come to her, and it was a poverdunce they did." That was her gentle sufferance and excuse.

Sarah had a lameness in her hip ; a good deal, indeed, was to be allowed for such a hindering infirmity. She made up for it with the agility of another little member, not meaning any harm, nor ever realizing that she could travel farther, on errand good or ill, in that fashion, than she could have done on her two feet.

The day came when things changed at Crooke Corner. Old Ephraim died.

One sunny afternoon in April the elbow of the road was filled with all sorts of carriages ; the one in which no creature rides but once drawn up in gloomy importance by the gate side.

The prayers were over, and the close knot of men about the door was broken up. People inside waited with deferent curiosity to see the mourners pass.

The bearing forth was accomplished, the single carriage was closed upon its occupant and crept away solemnly under the maples to halt beyond, while the living entered in turn their more cheerful vehicles. Foot passengers, who did not expect to "follow," departed slowly each way, up and down the road.

Two women talked as they walked along.

" Don't seem to me fun'ruls is so solumn or improvin 's they used to be," said one.

" Been to so many of 'em," said the other ; " got used to 'em."

" Well, I dun know. Live folks seem to get the upper hand of it, nowadays, somehow. The' 's only one dead one, you see, 'gainst 'em all ; an' the' 've all got their minds stirrin' full o' somethin'.

Folks is 'live, an' the times is hurryin', and they don't skeercely put it aside, more 'n while the prayers last, anyhow. Sometimes I kind o' think whether no they don't feel a little bit smart to *be* alive, an' walkin' off, speshully them that's pooty nigh o' the same age. There they go, like a parcel o' bees in a meddar, every one their own way, after their own honey. An' there goes old Iffrum Crooke, ridin' away alone, toes up."

" 'Randy Sowle did n't mind wearin' her new bunnit."

" No; did look ruther airy. But then folks don't dress accordin', as they used to, not even the mourners. 'Lizbuth Haven did n't have on a single stitch o' real black. Black silk gown 's nothin' ; an' there was little white flowers in the black lace on her bunnit."

" She 's only Mis' Crooke's niece. Wonder what they 'll do now ! Them two women all alone is pooty solitary. Don't see how they 'll manage, hardly. Old Iffrum used to shuffle round an' see to wood, an' water an' milk the cows ; an' I guess, off'n 's not, wash the pans an' cans. It 'll make a change, more or less."

It made two changes, one of which might have been easily anticipated ; the other nobody reckoned on. The Crookes hired a woman and a boy, and were better off than old Ephraim would ever have

thought they needed to be. And Miss Elizabeth
Haven came to board at the Corner.

People wondered, greatly relishing the sensation,
that Miss Haven should leave her beautiful city
rooms, where she had everything to her mind and
was in the middle of everything, to come out here
and fix up the old east wing and live a mile from
the cars with deaf Ma'am Crooke and lame Sarah.
But she had her reasons, which had been maturing
for some time against such possibility of acting
upon them as might occur, and now this had occurred. She wanted country air, — breath, both
bodily and spiritual. And she wanted to brighten
somebody's life, apart from associated charities,
which she found generalizing and depressing. Beside these facts, there was another in the shape
of a student at the neighboring law-school, young
Putnam King, whose mother had been Grace
Haven, Elizabeth's beautiful sister, who died when
Putnam was a baby. His father had married
again, and there was not only a kind, sensible step-
mother, but there had come a whole houseful of
young brothers and sisters, so that Putnam had not
devolved upon aunt Elizabeth's care or her affection, as left destitute of either. Neither did the
wise lady believe in any once-removed guardian-
ship, however tender, while real home ties and place
remained. But she loved the boy, and he loved

her as boys do, with a good deal of mischief and
bravado covering the feeling, and some looking-for
of auntly indulgence mixed up with it.

In these years of his absence from home for his
university training, aunt Elizabeth's rooms had
been pleasant to go to ; and as the time went
on and his future course determined itself and involved his remaining in the great city, she thought
of how good a thing it would be to establish
herself a little way out of it, far enough for a
thorough escape, and yet where he might come to
her for Sundays and holidays, into the sweet air
clean from woods and pastures ; that this would be
better for him than the droppings-in in town, which
were no change or renewal at all. She believed
in baptisms, and that the truth of them was at the
very heart of created things.

Putnam King demurred when she told him.

"You won't like it," he said. "You don't
know country people. They'll price your gowns
and calculate your 'means,' and they'll watch your
goings out and your comings in from this time
forth, forevermore."

"*Putnam*!"

"They will," rejoined Putnam, calmly. "They'll
know all your doings before they're done and all
your thoughts before you think 'em, and they
will mention to you any little circumstance or

change of your own as if it might be the first you 'd
ever heard of it. 'You 've got a new bonnet,'
'you 've lost a tooth, have n't yer?' or, 'you 're a
little grayer than you was last year, *ain't* yer?'
Oh, I know. They do down at Huxtable. I don't
dare to have my hair cut there. 'Hadger hair cut?'
Every man, woman and child I met observed that
to me one day. I fled to the garden and the
barn, and the hens began it. 'Hatcher ha' cut!
Hatcher ha' cut! 'Cher ha' cut, cut, cut, hatcher
ha' cut!' Everybody's affairs are forever in the
air. Everything chatters and every little chatter
is heard. It is the constitution of things in the
country. There 's no good, wholesome din of
everybody busy at once to hush things up. Oh,
you 'll get tired of it. You 'll wish you were a
trilobite."

"You absurd boy! But I 've a nice little room
for you there."

"I sha'n't come."

"You will; when you open your windows, it 's
into big trees full of birds."

"I told you so," said Putnam. "The little
birds of the air that carry the matter."

"And the sunrise comes in in the morning
straight across from the bay."

"Yes; everything is intrusive, and the sun and
the cows and the hens and the birds hustle you out

of your best nap. No, aunt; brick walls are more
to my morning mood, thank you."

" Well, then, I shall get rid of you."

" You'll get rid of yourself. You'll be pecked
into bits and you'll never be able to identify the
pieces; you'll never be a consistent entity any
more."

" You'll come to look after your own prophecy."

When Putnam King did come, and saw Sarah
Crooke and the old lady, his wonder and misdoubt
were at first the greater. But aunt Elizabeth's
rooms were like herself, more like her than ever,
with more space and freedom and sweetness to be;
and she was there, the same beautiful, consistent
entity as ever. And the fact accomplished was a
thing fit, on that side of the house, at least.

Putnam acknowledged it, so far. " But it's only
a question of time," he said. " You'll have to live
on yourself, even if the old maids don't eat you
up." He sat at the front window of Miss Haven's
pretty upstairs library, swinging the gray tassel of
her new holland blind to and fro, looking idly up
along the road as he spoke.

Miss Haven laughed in a very jolly way. " The
other old maids you mean, I suppose. But we
are n't all old maids. There's the minister, and
the doctor, and the doctor's wife and " —

But Putnam had stopped swinging the window tassel, and attending. He had turned away slightly, leaning forward as if he saw something. He drew back suddenly into the shelter of the curtain. "Come here, aunt Elizabeth. Who is this?" he said.

Just beyond the front corner of the west wing, a young girl stood upon the old stone wall. She had come running across the orchard and the field; her hair had fallen loose and she had her hat in her hand. Two other girls came along the street, laughing.

"Oh, wait, Sue! Connie, wait a minute! I've got away, but — ah!"

"So has your hair, hasn't it, and your breath?" said one of the newcomers, teasingly. "Everything gets away with you. Here, give me the hat; see how you're mashing the roses!" for the girl on the wall, with her last impatient ejaculation, had thrust her headgear under her elbow, where she held it anyhow, struggling with a hand and a half and one long pin to compress and fasten into a knot again a flowing mass of bonny brown locks with all the obstreperousness in them of natural kinks and curls.

"There! if it don't stay, I can't help it. I'm ready!" and she was jumping down from her perch upon two trim, pretty little feet, as three simultaneous remarks were being made about her in the old Crooke house.

"That's Rill Raye," answered aunt Elizabeth. "She lives on the North Road; she's just like her name, and as little to be hindered or quenched. And hindering and quenching are all that is tried upon her, I'm afraid."

"*Now* what prank do you s'pose that Rill Raye's ready for?" came up in Sarah Crooke's sharp, accusative accents from the west-side room below. Her "that" was an emphatically demonstrative pronoun.

"Do you know her? Speak to her, stop her, won't you? Ask her something!" The young man in the corner who objected theoretically to the sun and the birds and everything that was intrusive urged his sudden, eager curiosity upon aunt Elizabeth, holding himself well out of sight as he besought her hurriedly.

It suited aunt Elizabeth's own further purposes, and she did speak from the window. She had made up her mind, before this, to be friends somehow with Rill Raye.

"Are you going to the Point, to the library, Miss Raye?" she asked in her peculiarly clear voice that needed but slight raising to accomplish any attemptable distance. "Would you take a book for me?"

"Oh, with pleasure!" came Rill's answer. "Shall I come in for it, or will you drop it down?"

" Putnam — no, I 'll go myself," said Miss
Haven inside, as she took a brown-covered, red-
labeled volume from her round table, and hastened with it to the stairs. Putnam, for some
momentary preference of his own, sat still without
remonstrance.

Miss Haven, out upon the bank, held a brief
colloquy with the girl.

" You said you had ' got away,' " she began,
pleasantly. " Is there anything special to keep you
in just now ? All is well, I hope ? "

" Oh, yes ; only there 's always aunt Amelia,
and she thinks there are only two things life is good
for : weekdays, sew seams; Sundays, say hymns.
She thinks I am a little girl ; she will never be
done bringing me up, and I can't help growing,
that 's all. I always say hymns crooked, Miss
Haven. Is n't it funny ? "

The girls at the fence were listening. Rill
knew that, and it spurred her on. What would
have been the effect if she had known of the hidden auditor upstairs, cannot be certainly asserted ;
but, doubtless, she had a comfortable conviction
that behind some of those closed blinds there
might be other attentive ears which she had no
objection to startle. So she went on : —

" I do ; there 's a tother side to most of them.
Perhaps it 's the wrong side, but I don't know

always; it's hard to tell in some things. I turn
them over in my mind and hold them up to the
light — what light there is — as well as I can,-as
aunt Amelia turns new cloth to see which is the
right and the wrong of it; and presently I can't
tell one from the other any more than she can.
Do you remember ' How doth the little busy bee,'
Miss Haven?" The girl looked up in Miss
Haven's eyes with the most childlike simplicity.

" I think I do," returned the lady with a twin-
kling gravity.

" Well, I never got that settled yet," said Rill
Raye. " I always make it go this way : —

> ' That wretched little busy bee
> Spoils every pleasant minute ;
> He frets each opening flower to see
> If there is honey in it.'

He did when I was little, and he does now; and
all he wants is to lug the honey off and leave
the poor flower without any. Why should n't a
flower have its pretty, innocent blow-out its own
way, Miss Haven ? There would n't be any honey
in the world if it did n't. — Yes, I 'm coming,
girls. I was only explaining to Miss Haven that
we are meadowsweet and white clover on the ram-
page. — I 'll bring you back another book, Miss
Haven."

There was something very winning and gracious

in Rill Raye's way of repeating the name of the
person to whom she spoke, if an elder; unless, indeed, it happened to be Miss Crooke or one of her
sort, and then it was a satire simply because of objective absurdity. The manner was precisely the
same, but it was like taking off your hat to a
donkey or dropping a courtesy to a cow.

"You are very kind, Cyrilla. Miss Homer has
my list," returned Miss Haven, walking with Rill
the few steps across the grass-plot to the gate.
"May I just say something, dear? Some of the
sweetest flowers don't blow, they only quietly
bloom."

The girl's eyes had something suddenly deeper
in them as she looked up in Miss Haven's.

"When they grow in still, nice, sunshiny places,"
she said, wistfully.

"They grow in their own spots where they are
put, and they make them beautiful. They do not
try to rush about or transplant themselves."

"But they reach their blossoms through the
fences, — they must reach somewhere."

Rill had the last word; perhaps it was wisdom
in Miss Haven that she left it with her.

When she came back and stopped with the book,
Miss Haven met her as before. But Cyrilla was
very quiet this time, and she looked pale. She
handed the volume over the gate without speaking.

"Has anything happened? Don't you feel well? Come in a minute," the lady said, kindly.

Cyrilla shook her head. "I 've had a tooth pulled, that 's all," she answered, briefly, and with the slight facial constraint natural to the circumstance. I 'll come to-morrow, — may I?"

There was an appeal in the word. Miss Haven laid her hand on Rill's with a kind pressure, "Do," she said. "Come any time. This is Dropping-in Corner, you know."

Rill's handkerchief lightly hid her mouth, but her eyes smiled. It was a smile with a pathos in it. "I 'm just as full of mischief and mistakes as I can be," she said. "I want to be done ever so much good to, but " — and the flash of fun came back again — "I *don't* want to be *amelia*rated!"

"There 's the making of a splendid woman in that girl," said Miss Haven, coming back to Putnam King in her bookroom. "She has been following some joke or daring to the bitter end. She never started for it, I am sure."

"Started for what?" asked Putnam. "What happened to her to wilt her down so?"

"She had a tooth pulled. Dr. Harriman is a young D. D. S. just established at the Point, — a handsome man, a gentleman. Some nonsense of those other girls, and Rill Raye has paid up the cost of the frolic. I feel sure of it."

pletons, the other was Miss Rill Raye. She is proud and quick; she found out she was in the wrong place and had the pluck to right herself. One of the simpletons began. She wanted to let me see her teeth, she said. She smiled, and showed a very pretty row of them. I very nearly thanked her, but I bowed, and waited orders. The quick one — I did n't know her name then — saw right through me, — that *I* was seeing through, and her great dark eyes flashed. The other girl, as innocent as you please, put up her lip with her finger. 'Is n't there a speck there, somewhere?' she wanted to know. I did n't care about playing uncle Toby, but I had to look. There was a speck there; I believe she had stuck it on herself. A touch with a probe point removed it. 'I do not think you need me,' I said. 'Your *teeth* appear to be in perfect order.' The dark-eyed one caught the emphasis, and flashed again. 'Is this all, young ladies?' I inquired, taking in the committee of three that had been requisite for this mighty business. '*No, sir!*' came like a small bombshell from Miss Raye. 'I wish to have a tooth taken out.' And before I could say Ah! she had whipped her hat off and was in the chair. The others were staring. One made a little shriek. Miss Raye twisted herself round. 'If you mean to scream,' said she, 'please go away. I don't.' Well, the amount of it was, the tooth needed to come out, though she had n't had the smallest intention that it should, up to the instant. Then she did order me: 'Pull it, doctor. You know it ought to be done; I was told to have it out a year ago.' A very slight filling would have preserved it, but it was an irregularity in an otherwise fine mouth, and it crowded perniciously. I did it, that's all."

"I see," returned Miss Haven. "Thank you. I like to have the story from its root. You know, Dr. Harriman, how a little thing gets circulated, and takes character in the circulation. I live at Crooke Corner; I hear most things; and I take an interest in Rill Raye. Good-morning; perhaps you will find it in your way some time to call in upon an old friend of your mother's?"

Dr. Harriman bowed, expressed his sense of the privilege and his acceptance, and attended her to the door, returning into his office with not a little enlightenment as to the social trend of things in Wewachet.

Rill Raye told her aunt Amelia the simple fact that she had had the tooth drawn. She scorned concealment.

Aunt Amelia uttered a sharp "H'm!" She wondered how long it would have been before Rill would have made up her mind to let old Dr. Grapleigh do it; blamed her, upon sudden recollection,

as the girl had expected, for going without consult-
ing herself, or being properly accompanied ; and
taxed her outright with having had no real purpose
but to make an interesting acquaintance with the
new handsome young practitioner. " Of course
he saw through it quick enough," she said, sting-
ingly. " And what do you suppose he thought of
a girl who would do that ? "

" He thought I meant what I said, aunt Amelia ;
I might have got his advice, and put it off, as I did
Dr. Grapleigh's. I don't trouble myself at all
about what he thinks."

" Yes, you do. You 've done a foolish thing, and
you know it. It 's in the tip of your head, this
minute. You 'll have to be ashamed of it every
time you see him."

It was in this sort that Miss Amelia Bonable
punished the young woman whom she thought sin-
cerely she was dealing with in rare wisdom.

The tip of the head was emphasized.

" I am not ashamed, and I shall not see him,"
the girl answered with extreme loftiness. " I do
not know Dr. Harriman. I do not remember him
in the least except that he — that I — employed
him."

CHAPTER II.

THERE was something, after all, in Rill Raye, that made her capable of learning her own life-lessons. She had got one now, although she denied it, even to herself; yet she would run just as headlong into some other experience and invite the wholesome bitterness of that.

Rill Raye kept her word. Dr. Harriman met her in the street, and was about to raise his hat; his look arrested itself and his hand moved upward for the infinitesimal part of an instant and for an inch of space. There gesture and expression were checked by the unrecognition apparently too serenely thorough to be a cut, upon a face that neither swerved from him as it went by, nor met his glance with the most involuntary consciousness. If she had planned this next step with the deepest coquetry, perhaps she could not have managed better.

"I wonder how she got that up?" was the doctor's mental exclamation. There was a half-smile upon his lips as he walked on, diverted and stimulated to interest by this little problem.

She had simply made up her mind that for her, under present circumstances, Dr. Harriman did not exist.

Meanwhile, she had been to see Miss Haven, as she had desired and promised, and Miss Haven had been to see her aunt Amelia.

Miss Bonable did not know what to do with the girl, she said. She came to this point of confidence with Miss Haven to her own surprise; hardly perceiving that it was because Miss Haven spoke kindly of Rill. When people commented on her in a different sort, Miss Bonable was ready, as she said, to "brussle up;" unconscious also that this was in itself more harmful than helpful, as revealing a touchy sensitiveness. But when Miss Haven said nice things, the simple perplexity spoke itself out, and found relief.

"She's careless, and she don't care. And she will have her own way," said aunt Amelia, not intending either paradox or repetition. She meant that Rill was idle, untidy, according to her ideas of method and industry, and that she did care, emphatically, to do as she pleased.

"Why, she won't mend her second-best gown till the best is torn too, and as for stockings, or making up anything new beforehand, why, you might as well talk to that kitten! Only the other day, I bought her some real pretty summer stuff at the mark-down price. 'Now,' says I, 'you don't really want it this season; but why don't you go to work and make it up, and lay it away for next spring? Then you'll be forehanded when the warm weather comes all of a jump.' And what do you think she answered back? 'I guess I'd need to be *four*handed, to do all you'd like me to do,' says she. 'And what do I want to waste this summer for, working for next? Why, next summer I might be — a widow!' The first thing comes into her head comes off her tongue, let it be whatever!"

"She's a bright girl," said Miss Haven.

"Bright? Yes, and smart, too, when she does take hold. If it were n't mostly the things she'd ought to let alone. But I don't praise her; nor let her see that I laugh, if she *is* funny. And I don't scold. The only way is to touch her pride; she's got that; and I mortify her." Miss Bonable shook out her work and set up her head, and fixed her lips in a grim certainty of astute righteousness.

"Oh, you can't mean to do that! Why, to mortify is to make *dead*, you know," said Miss Haven, quickly, yet sweetly. "I would n't *mortify* anybody, not even a dumb creature. That *does* put down, beyond reach."

"Well, I d' know. There's got to be some dis-

cipline. And she's eighteen years old. I can't slap her, nor put her in the closet."

"We are all apt to mistake punishment for discipline. Discipline is teaching. The Lord shows us our good as well as our evil."

Miss Bonable did not say anything. This of itself was a remarkable effect with her.

"Rill is a brave girl, too," Miss Haven adventured.

"Oh, you've heard that, have you?" Miss Bonable rejoined quickly, her head going up again as with a spring, and her hand, with her needle in it, held arrested in high air. "I knew it would travel. That's what I told her."

"You mean, I suppose, her having her tooth drawn. That is only one thing. She told me that herself, merely as a statement. I guessed the bravery of it."

"Other folks will guess the accounting-for of the bravery. There's always talk."

"Yes, there always is. Human beings take an interest in each other. That is why it is well to meet talk with talk, or to anticipate. I think we ought to take pains to say all the best we can of each other, since something is sure to be said."

"You'll have chance enough to try that at Crooke Corner," said Miss Bonable. "Perhaps it'll work, if you can get your sort of word in edgeways. But I guess it 'll come in kind o' flat, like bread-sauce without pepper or onion."

" I hope I may make good my opportunity. And there are things in character, as in bread-sauce, that would be intolerable by themselves, but are relishing as condiments."

" I should n't wonder if some of your resates might make the world taste better than it does," said Miss Bonable, dropping her work and getting up to see her visitor to the door, as the latter moved to go. And Miss Haven knew, by the tone and motion, that she was leaving a little new courage behind her, in a spirit anxious with difficulties, and hard because of anxieties.

Miss Haven went straight from Miss Bonable's over to Mrs. Rospey's. There was word in the village that Mrs. Rospey was left without a girl again. Girls at Mrs. Rospey's were always flaring up and leaving. The lady had a doubtful name among her acquaintances, as " one who was always changing," and a very decided and detrimental one in the kitchen constituency, as " hard to get along with." " You won't stay a week at Rospey's," was the common saying in the solidarity. Prophecy fulfilled itself. Cause and effect acted and reacted, until you could n't tell which began it. Girls went to Mrs. Rospey's as with a loaded revolver, all ready to fire at the first move. It was

"hands up!" from the start. Poor Mrs. Rospey
was helpless. Amiability itself could not save her.
After a brief space of relief and of Christian hope
that she was beginning to keep her temper and
should keep her girl, down came the thunderbolt
out of the clear sky, and the Katie or Annie of
the time "gave notice." The secret which the
mistress did not penetrate was, that, not expecting
to stay more than "a week at Rospey's," the in-
cumbent was simply there *in transitu ;* saving
board and doing her washing, making ready for a
place to which she had been pledged beforehand,
and in which she did expect to stay as long as
"things were agreeable." And if friends knew
of any thoroughly good person to fill the duties,
they thought it less than useless to make the suggestion in Mrs. Rospey's behalf, from the difficulty
of persuasion on the one side, and the difficulty
of knowing when she was well off on the other.
"You can't stop a leak with water," they said.

"What is it this time?" was the question that
went about, when a fresh vacancy was reported.
And this time — of Miss Haven's visit — it had
been, as currently asserted, the throwing of a dishcloth in the servant's face. "And you could n't
expect anybody to stand that," was the appended
comment. What might have happened first, that
Mrs. Rospey could n't be expected to stand, was
never inquired.

One of Miss Haven's rules was " not to talk *round* a person." She knew very well she could hear the whole dishcloth story at Mrs. Clackett's, or Mrs. Wisper's ; but she did not care at all about the dishcloth ; she was a more thorough gossip, she sometimes said to Sarah Crooke, than to be interested in what everybody knew, and had repeated threadbare ; the real zest of a subject was in the point unreached and hardest to get at. If she could n't find out a little more than her neighbors, it was n't worth while to gossip at all. When, therefore, a hearsay came trickling along to her, she did not drink of it with all that it might have gathered on its way ; neither did she even paddle in it, or stir it up, to send it further a little more roiled then before. If she did anything, she followed it straight up to the springhead, and saw for herself with what quality it started. In this case, in the midst of the bubbling and boiling, she found a flavor sweeter than she had even hoped.

The bereaved housekeeper was brushing down her front staircase when Miss Haven rang at the door. Mrs. Rospey's face brightened as she let her visitor in, and led the way to a dainty little sitting-room.

" I wish the Lord would give me a new set of nerves ! " she said, after making due explanation of her employment and of her big morning apron.

" Perhaps He will — by providing a good rest for
the old ones," returned Miss Haven.

" Ah, you know all about it," exclaimed Mrs. Rospey, gratefully, " and of course you know the old
ones stand in the way of my getting it. It seems
as if the Lord himself could n't make out which
end to begin at."

" I came to tell you of a very nice woman who is
just left out of a place. She never *left* one in her
life."

" She 'd better not come here, then. She 'd
break her record. She would n't stay. They
never do. She would n't *come* if she 's principled
against leaving.

" The minute anything goes contrary, they tell
me they knew it would, — they were warned they
could n 't live with me. — and all I want is that
they should do things with some sort of conscience.
If I liked to have the kitchen sweepings, dust and
ashes and bones and lemon-skins, piled up behind
the coal-hod, and half the breakfast thrown into
the scrap-pail, and the glass-towels used to wipe
the stove, and the napkins for oven cloths, I could
get along beautifully. I should be easy to live
with : but I should n't live easy with myself. I
found the last one washing out the soup-pot with a
doily, and I snatched it out of her hand and flung
it across to the kitchen table ; but it had to go past

her on the way, and she said I threw it at her. I
know it was temper, and it was n't dignified ; but
I don't believe Moses could be dignified — or
meek — if he had to regulate such things with
such creatures. When he *did* lose his temper, he
smashed all the ten commandments."

Mrs. Rospey laughed hysterically ; and then the
tears sprung in her eyes and trembled in her voice.
It was partly the understanding look in Miss Haven's face, and the sympathy of her smile. " Why,
I 've *prayed* about it," she went on, putting her
hand out and laying it on her friend's ; " and then
I 've gone straight downstairs and found something
I could n't stand, and knew I *ought n't* to stand,
and I 've upset the whole calabash again."

" You are too good a housekeeper, perhaps, to be
easily a temper-keeper."

" *Ought n't* I to be a good housekeeper ? " demanded Mrs. Rospey, with earnest eyes. She was
only thirty, yet ; and thirty is young in the intri-
cacies of experience.

" Set one ought against another," suggested Miss
Haven.

" It 's only double-ought, after all ; it makes it
just a hundred times as hard. I *ought* to take
good care of things, and I *ought* to be kind to people. I *can* do them separately ; but when it 's people and things together, people that ought to help

me with the things " — She broke down with her speech in a tangle.

" Yes ; there 's that ought on the other side," said Miss Haven. " Lucretia Dawse would fill it. She is at Shepaug. If I come for you to-morrow morning, will you drive there with me and see her ? "

" Yes. And I 'll tell her just what she 's got to put up with. For I 'm all nerves now, of the wrong sort ; and I sha'n't be easy-going all at once. But you — what did you come for — to help me so ? "

" Oh, I only came gossiping. But I guess it was an errand. We don't always know when we are sent — till we get there. I shall be glad if this turns out a comfort."

" It *has* turned out a comfort," said Mrs. Rospey. " And it 's good to have somebody *come* gossiping, and find out the sense of your affairs. It 's a new way."

Before Miss Haven got home that day, she had added two more items to her budget of interior information.

She found out that the minister 's wife did *not* spend a quarter part of that last reception present in new satin covers for her parlor chairs : but that she had reseated them herself with the odd breadths of an ancient damask gown out of an old family trunk, of exactly the rich, sober brown that her eyes loved, and of an obsolete, honest, indestructible stuff.

And then the good lady met Colonel Sholto, who had married the pretty young widow March, riding with his stepson. He sent the boy on at a canter, and stopped Miss Haven to say something to her about a book-club. But first he pointed after the little fellow with his whip. "Takes to the saddle well, does n't he?" he said, with as much pride as a real father could.

Miss Haven nodded, with a pleased look, along the line of direction. "You've made him happy with a pony, then?" she said.

"Yes. It's better than the stable yards. Jack's of good stuff, but good stuff might be spoiled in the handling. Do you know what he said to me at the beginning of our concerns with each other?"

Colonel Sholto had not the least idea that she could; his "do you know?" was merely preliminary. Miss Haven surprised him by saying she had heard something odd; but would he please tell her himself? She was fond of a good story, and always liked to get the whole of it.

"What did you hear?"

"That he marched up to you and stated that his mother might have a step-husband if she wanted to, but that he would n't be a step-boy to anybody."

Colonel Sholto gave a quick, big-chested laugh.
"Nearly verbatim," he replied.

"What did you say?" asked Miss Haven.

Colonel Sholto's face grew graver and very pleasant as he answered: "I told him that was spirited;
and good, in the best sense of it. I hoped there
would be no half relations with any of us; I meant
to be his friend, and should want him for mine;
and we must *both* stand up for his mother. He
had the quickness and honesty to take home that
last hint; I could see it by his color; but his eyes
gave me the right look, and — well, I think we *are*
friends, Miss Haven."

"Thank you."

"I don't know why I have told you all this,
right here in the street; but there was something
in your face that went beyond the first word, and
so you have it."

"Thank you," said Miss Haven again. "There
is always something beyond the first word. The
first word hardly ever satisfies me."

There was that in her response which went
beyond the word also. Colonel Sholto felt it,
and was glad they had spoken. After all, he
rode away, forgetting what he first had stopped
for.

When Elizabeth Haven got home, she took off
her bonnet in Sarah Crooke's parlor before going

upstairs. She had a way of doing this; she knew that Sarah Crooke liked it.

"Well, what have you picked up?" was the stereotyped query.

"Some dropped stitches," said Miss Haven. "They piece out several things. Miss Bonable thinks pretty well of Kill Raye, to begin with. She says she's bright, and proud, and capable, and self-respecting. She can always influence her through her self-respect."

Miss Sarah opened her eyes wide.

"She has so *much* character, that it makes her anxious about dealing with her just right."

"Don't say!" interjected Miss Sarah.

"Yes; that's just what I do say, just what I wanted to have to say. It's a little more than most folks know."

This view of the matter evidently struck Miss Sarah, for she stopped knitting in the middle of her needle, and replied nothing.

"And I 've been to Mrs. Rospey's," Miss Haven went on; "and the dishcloth was a damask napkin that she took away in a hurry from the girl who was cleaning a kettle with it. The rest of the story was of the girl's authorship; and a sweeter, tenderer little woman than Mrs. Rospey — inside — I don't believe there is in Wewachet. I 'm going to send Lucretia Dawse to her. She wants

somebody of her own sort. Her house is like wax-
work. When there are birds of a feather, there 'll
be peace in the nest."

" Well, I declare ! You do seem to have got the
inside track ! I never had any objections to Martha Rospey ; but she 's been awful quick-tempered
in her kitchen — alwers."

" It 's good to know the whole of a thing," said
Miss Haven, quietly. " And then I met Colonel
Sholto, riding with Jack March. He has given
the little fellow a pony, and he told me that
he and Jack made friends from the minute the
boy told him he would n't be step-boy to anybody.
Colonel Sholto said he did n't want any half relations, and I guess it 's a whole one now, at any
rate."

" He told you all that — a-horseback ! I guess
you follered him up pretty close. I thought you
was n't inquisitive."

" Oh, yes, I am ; as inquisitive as Eve, only I
like my information from the best authority. I
should n't accept the serpent's account of a thing.
It is remarkable how much more people know
about themselves sometimes than you can tell them.
Mrs. Pinceley's chairs are made out of her great-
aunt's old ironside gown ; she seated them herself,
and they look as if they were born so, with satin
skins."

"Seems to me everything 's got a satin skin, or *you* 've new covered 'em. You 're a dabster at perticklers, anyhow."

"Cousin Sarah," said Elizabeth Haven, very cordially, " you have a wonderful opportunity in your life, I think. Everybody comes to you, and you are interested about everybody. You could generally know more than any one else; and you have a clear judgment, and chance to weigh and consider. You could set ever so many things straight in Wewachet. "

"Can't make folks over. They will tattle, and they like things best before they 're all explained. After they 've wondered awhile, they 'll take the explanation, may be. *That* 's something new, then. But they will have the *new*." Miss Sarah said "ni-ew," and it was very effective. "I 'm bound to say I like the ni-ew myself," she repeated, with the honesty Miss Haven provoked from almost everybody.

"We all like it. We 're made to like it. There would n't be any growing or getting on if we did n't. But in the matter of talk about other people, I think there are just three rules that make it safe, and leave us all the interest and satisfaction."

"I 'd be pleased to know 'em. I 'd be pleased to hear of any rules that folks would be likely to talk by. You can't even keep 'em to dictionary and grammar," said Miss Sarah Crooke.

"They are very simple," said Miss Haven. "To tell the best things; to make the best of the bad things; and to straighten the mistakes."

"That's all very pretty, and very well for you, who can get about and root things out; but I set here in my corner and take what comes."

"It seems to me that is the opportunity. It seems to me it is like a call," said Miss Haven, in her way that went behind the word she answered.

Sarah Crooke twinkled. "Like Matthoo at the resate o' custom?" she asked.

"Something so, perhaps."

"I can't build up a ni-ew world — nor yet make a millennium — stuck here like a limpet!"

"I don't suppose we have to think of the millennium," Miss Haven answered; "only of each little million-millionth of the right at a time. When the Lord made the mollusk He did n't say, 'Go to work and build a continent.' But every little mollusk grew his shell the best and truest shape he could, and lived his life out; and the continent gathered together, and rose under the water, till the Lord's own time came, and He lifted it up into the light."

"You're a good talker, and you've got a good

headpiece," said Sarah Crooke, as she fell to knitting again with a force that hinted a climax to the conversation. Miss Haven accepted both compliment and hint with a smile, took her bonnet, and went off upstairs.

CHAPTER III.

PUTNAM KING professed great delight in his
aunt's shrewd reformatory proceedings. " How do
you get along with your new School for Scandal ? "
he would ask, when he came out to Wewachet for
a Saturday to Monday stay. " It is the greatest
woman-movement yet. But it interferes with their
dearest rights, I 'm afraid. Does n't it take the
edge off life for Sarah Crooke ? "

" Now, Putnam, look here! Sarah Crooke has
a fine background to her character."

" Why does she keep it in the background, I
wonder!" interpolated Putnam; but Miss Haven
went sturdily on.

" If *you* were tied to an armchair and four
knitting-needles, — no, we will say to a pipe and a
newspaper, — you — or any man — would be a
thousand times worse gossip than ever she was.
Would be? You are now; and your newspapers
are your condemnation. You *men*, you *devourers*
of news, to despise gossip! when the daily columns

don't suffice for you, with all their biggest capitals, and life is bare, unless the world comes to a partial end every day to feed your voracity ! "

" Oh, that 's legitimate," said Putnam, laughing. " It 's published news; it concerns the world, — we don't want it upside down, but we must know if it is ; it 's important. And print is open to contradiction and refutation. It 's responsible. It does n't keep its tail in a hole, like an earthworm, ready to draw back if it sees danger."

" Oh, does n't it ? Putnam King, newspaper gossip is the very crown — no, abyss — of gossip ! See here ! Did n't I read only the other day, in one of your high-toned journals, a long screed on one side about what the American newspaper is doing toward the bringing up of the American small boy in the way he should n't go ; a virtuous, holy-horror article against the stuff with which the press had been bursting for days about a prize fight and the fighters ; and did n't I turn over the sheet and come pat upon an Associated Press report from New Orleans of this same prize fight, a column and a half long, with every punch and bruise of every round in it ? And over the top — tail in a hole, to be sure — just the salvo of protest in a line of the heading —' SHAMEFUL AFFAIR ! ' Oh, *tail in a hole !* As if that line, in such enormous print, were n't the very crier's bell to sell the paper by ! "

The good lady paused for breath, just gasping for the third time, with triple-X scorn, — " Tail in a hole, truly ! "

Putnam King gasped with merriment. Then he put on a serene, judicial air, mingled with benevolent instructiveness, and said : —

" Two different departments, auntie ! Two separate worms. The regular Associated Press takes its course ; then the editorial comes in with comments. But you 're right, in a way. It 's like conduct and conscience. It 's human warious, that 's all."

" It 's masculine warious. Women have n't got all the human nature. That 's what I said. Anyway, the papers are n't fit to touch. and you have to read them with your eyes shut. If women's talk is any worse than that ! "

" Aunt Elizabeth, you 're a merciful-minded person ; but when you do sit down on a thing, you sit down hard ! "

" I 've got the slips. I cut them out and kept them," Miss Elizabeth persisted, calmly holding on to her facts.

" Never mind. Be good and change the subject. Tell me something about Miss Rill Raye," said the young man, audaciously.

" Won't you please give me your special definition of gossip ? " asked Miss Haven, opening her eyes wide at him, and dropping her words singly and slowly, with a calm sarcasm. " The thing old women are prone to, and men and the newspapers decline ? "

" Personal talk, I suppose, without sympathy or necessity. But don't ask me to define the sympathy, or argue the necessity. Tell me about Miss Raye ! "

" She was here the other night to tea," Miss Haven answered, curtly.

" Why is it always the *other* night ? " demanded the young man, with an absurd tone of injury.

Miss Haven found it difficult to distinguish between his chaff and his earnest ; or rather, perhaps, to find out whether the chaff covered any bit of earnest she might deprecate. She had taken care not to bring these two young persons together, chiefly because she would not let another story be begun about Rill Raye ; also because she wanted to have her freely to herself for awhile.

" I do not want all my company on the same night," she said. " We had a thunderstorm."

" Was that a foregone conclusion ? Part of the company ? "

" Do you ask from sympathy or necessity ? "

" Both. I am really concerned for a young woman who carries such meteorological conditions with her, and I might guide my own arrivals by the

weather bureau. Would it have been any more
thundery if you had had more company?"

Aunt Elizabeth was pretty sure it was all chaff.
The pretense of interest was too out-thrust and exaggerated to have in it any touch of dangerous
reality. Here was where the limitation of her
judgment showed itself, and played her false. She
determined for a man upon feminine premises. So
she fell into the snare again, and gave him, as she
had done on other occasions, all the little piquan-
cies and illustrations of her latest study of Rill
Raye. She brought the two together, all unaware,
much more nearly than if she had invited them to
tea expressly at the same time.

"Don't talk such stilted nonsense," she remon-
strated, and forthwith launched into her little
story; which, as Putnam did immediately dismiss
his stilted nonsense and become an unobstructive
listener, I will put, if you please, in my own way,
as a part of mine.

Miss Haven had two main principles in her system of social diplomacy which she was trying to
work out here in Wewachet, and specially with
Sarah Crooke. First, she believed in bringing
people nearer to each other. She knew how either
closeness or remoteness influences feeling; how a
certain forced isolation gives a sense of injury and
deprivation; how sympathy is warped to criticism,

and criticism tends to cruelty. Social inaccessibility is like that which prompts the gunner's impulse to bring down the bird. The same hand which pulls the trigger might tenderly nurse a frightened, wounded thing that fluttered to it for help or shelter; but the thing beyond, in its own element, reachable by no direct and natural touch, is a mark for eager hunting down and bringing near as prey. Miss Haven often found, as her theory argued, that to fetch inside of range was to save from the weapon's aim.

In the second place, she reasoned and discovered that one may touch the very nerve of gossipy desire, the palate of its hunger, to some nobler satisfying by finding choicer, rarer bits than the common menu furnished. So she brought home to Sarah Crooke, eager and famishing in her deprived corner, both people and things.

Instead of letting Rill Raye go by, and Sarah sit wondering where she had been or whither might be bound, on what errand of madcapry, — or mantrapry, as would better have expressed her idea of Rill's bits of fun and flirting, — Miss Haven asked the girl in, and kept her to tea ; letting her use her bright nonsense in amusing Miss Sarah, who, with all her animadversions, dearly loved to be made to laugh, and with her frank gossip about herself anticipate and disarm all guesswork and tattle.

Not infrequently some incident called forth a brave kindliness, a gentle generosity, a ready service, which were in Rill's nature, and which surprised a pleasure and gratitude from Sarah Crooke that were, at least, next door to affection.

On this summer afternoon in question, Rill had come up from the Point and stopped in to find Miss Haven just returned from town, and inclined to make scrap-holiday by some pleasant sort of doing nothing. "Come down into the orchard," she said to Rill. "Talk to Miss Sarah, and play bézique with me, and then take tea with us."

Miss Haven's steamer-chair had been carried down among the apple-trees, where she had beguiled cousin Sarah into a habit of sitting in the pleasant weather, under the low arches of the old boughs borne downward in the gracious shaping of their long fruit bearing. Three or four of these broad shelters were grouped in the hollow of the field, where the breeze moved more softly than on the land-swell; and here each lady had chosen her own customary place, apart, and yet near enough for talk and companionship. Hither, now, Miss Haven and Rill brought cards and lapboard. Nothing rested Miss Elizabeth like a simple game, she said; she could not sit still and fold her hands, there was too much main force in that; so with Sarah Crooke she played cribbage, or cassino, or, with Rill Raye, the more intricate bézique.

The old lady, Sarah's mother, did not come out; she rarely left her armchair now. "She'd gi'en up runnin' outdoor," she said, "long ago; she thought Sarah was most too old a girl for such capers." She was growing much more deaf, and "sence Radne came, and was so kind o' comfortin' and easy with her, she didn't seem to care for change, or even visitin'." She had established herself and her gray knitting-work within her little "kitchen bedroom," by the window at the bed-head. Often her only movement was from the one resting-place to the other. "Seemed someway," she said, "'s though she couldn't rest enough." Poor thing; she had done over-hours' work all her life. Sarah was a good daughter; her "beautiful eye" was always turned upon her mother; she would go and sit by her the hour together, laboriously repeating to her the news, and answering her reiterated questions; but doubtless it was a respite to escape at intervals into the freshness and liberty devised for her by cousin Elizabeth.

Miss Haven had brought a bunch of flowers from Mrs. Sholto, with that lady's kind remembrance for Miss Crooke. Miss Haven and Mrs. Sholto had driven together from the station, and the latter had made the carriage wait at her door while she fetched a handful of greenhouse blooms from some bowl freshly filled with them, vivid in beauty from their summering in open-air borders.

" My cousin will so like them," Miss Haven had said with her thanks ; and then Mrs. Sholto had answered graciously, " Give them to her with my kind remembrance."

Sarah Crooke had taken them with a delight accentuated by the unexpected personal attention. " They drive by, and drive by," she had said to herself often, " and never know or care that there are any bodies in the plain old houses on the way, or any souls in the bodies."

Now, unawares, by a simple, single act, a seal — or an anointing to charity — was laid upon the the querulous lips again, and a new individual indemnity was secured against unfavoring " they say's " with Sarah Crooke. She had this sterling good about her : she could not talk, or think, two ways ; though either of her only two ways was sufficiently decided. Miss Haven played carefully upon the right string ; she talked herself, she liked to. " An old maid must chatter," she said ; " but a Christian woman need not spatter."

She talked a good deal elsewhere about cousin Sarah ; always " cousin ; " and people knew better than they had ever done before what had got shut up and hidden away by her disabilities. She brought her own visitors over into Miss Sarah's room, and presently they began to inquire at the door for " the ladies." At first it was to please

Miss Haven; then it pleased themselves to see how they could give pleasure to one so deprived; and the discovery of her harmlessness lent the fascination that is found in approaching some creature supposed dangerous, but proving gentle.

" It 's a good, still afternoon for outdoors," said Miss Crooke, contentedly. Miss Haven had been to the bank and the broker's for her, in the city, and had brought out to her some mortgage interest, and the cash for a check, and her bank-book. These Miss Sarah was looking over, as she lay back easily in the long chair, with her feet upon the rest under an afghan. " No wind to pester these things, or the cards."

" Four kings — eighty ! " called Rill, in her clear young voice, triumphantly.

" And four queens," responded Miss Haven, putting up her score.

" You always have the queens, and I the kings," said Rill, as they played on. " No ; ten and a royal marriage ! You played right into my hand. But have n't you forgotten to put up your own bézique ? A hundred for aces, and sixty for queens, and you were two hundred and fifty ; yes, you ought to be at the ninety. You don't look out for yourself half the time." And so the deals and the game went on.

Miss Crooke had read over her papers, and

counted her bank-bills, and put them back into
the envelope; then she pushed all down carefully
into a deep, brown silk bag, whose strings she
drew close and tied in a knot, placing the whole
under her cushion; after which, with a serene
mind, she listened awhile to the bézique announce-
ments, inwardly counting up a different set of
figures which belonged to the comfortable little
investments and deposits she had been reviewing;
and so, gradually, fell fast asleep.

"How hot it grows!" said Rill Raye.

"Yes; this stillness is like a blanket: but it is
quite shady; the sun has gone in."

"I should think it had! Miss Haven, turn
round and look at that cloud!"

A low, black heap was rolling steadily over from
the westward. A wind was behind it that would
come here presently. Under the trees the shadow
thickened fast. Every bird had hidden in some
leafy nook. There was not a sound nor a stir, except their own movement and voices.

"It will be here in three minutes. We must
get cousin Sarah in."

The cards were shuffled together, and dropped
upon the chair from which Miss Haven had hurriedly arisen.

As she came to Miss Crooke's side, a swift flash
shot from the blackness that mounted overhead; a

quivering dazzle of flame wrapped air and earth in an instant's frightful illumination, and a crash of thunder fell like an avalanche.

Miss Crooke, startled from sleep, — afraid of lightning even when under shelter, hardly able to gain her feet, and wholly helpless to hasten, — was nearly paralyzed with the shock of terror.

CHAPTER IV.

" INTRODUCE ME."

Radne came running to the women in the orchard, her apron over her head, for flimsy defense, while the big raindrops drove like bullets, solid and far apart, straight down among them to the ground.

" Why, ain't you all crazy, I should like to know ! " she ejaculated, rushing to the rescue. She took Miss Crooke right up into her arms, and fled staggering back with her. The others brought what they could, and followed. But the brown silk bag fell, forgotten for the instant in the scurry, as Miss Haven seized pillow and afghan from the chair.

For the first few minutes of the tempest, when hail began to dash against the window panes with almost shattering force, and the outside world palpitated from blaze to blackness with the rapidity of some gigantic nictitation, nobody thought of any little accessory thing. Yet when Miss Sarah did cry out, " Oh, my money and my papers ! " the dismay of the serious mischance added itself, not without a touch of absurd Shakesperean association, to the panic of the storm.

Cushions and wraps were tossed over and shaken. The great brown silk bag was not among them. "My ducats," or their representatives, nowhere appeared.

"They 'll all be paper-mill pulp! Oh, my gracious, what a flash! We 'll all be killed, and I sha'n't have a cent o' money left to live on!"

Not one of the other women noticed that Rill Raye had slipped out of the room. They all stumbled against each other, and flapped things in each other's faces. Before they missed the girl she stood among them again, with rain-wet face and locks, and garments heavily dashed with water.

"Here it is," she said quietly, and held out the recovered treasure to Miss Sarah.

"The Lord and the land!" cried that astonished woman. "You ain't ben down that orchard in this flame and fury!"

"It did n't take three minutes," Rill answered coolly.

Somehow their fears laid themselves down before her bravery. They were calm and still after that; only now and again Sarah Crooke would ejaculate, "Well, I 'm beat! I have n't got a word to say! Rill Raye, you come and sit by me," she

commanded, when they drew up at last for such a
repast as they could make without the agency of
the cooking-stove, which was approached only for
a hurried filling of a pitcher with boiling water
for their tea. They drank it without spoons, and
they ate short biscuit and sponge cake without
knives and forks, for the livid lightning still
streamed and pulsed, and the rain beat and thunder rent with those occasional splitting sounds that
told of some material thing that had made a link
between angry sky and trembling earth.

Radne had helped Mrs. Crooke to bed. " They 'd
better all go," the old lady had said tremulously.
"Make 'em all go to bed, Radne. If the' 's any
place safe, it 's feathers." Radne had closed the
wooden shutters in the bedroom, and brought a
light ; then the simple soul, hidden away and not
seeing the storm any longer, quieted down and fell
asleep.

" It 's set in for a night of it. You can't get
home," said Sarah Crooke to Rill. The latter was
resuming her boots, that had been slid across the
kitchen floor by Radne to a drying-place beneath
the stove, and replaced by a big pair of flannel
shoes belonging to Miss Sarah.

" I must. Aunt Amelia will have been awfully
frightened, and if I don't get back she won't sleep
a wink all night."

" It can hardly last like this," said Miss Haven.
" And if anything can get about, the express will
come with my parcels from town. We can send
word over by Thrape."

" I can go with Thrape," said Rill, simply.

Miss Sarah Crooke had a sudden insight of how
it came to pass, perhaps, that this girl was apt to
do queer things. Methods were indifferent when
motive was controlling, and henceforth, she thought,
she would trust her for some decent sort of motive
in almost anything.

Rill did go home with Thrape, riding by his
side on the high front seat of his heavy covered
wagon ; the storm still flashing and growling, and
renewing itself suddenly at intervals.

" And she don't know but half his load is crowbars and cooking-stoves. He carries everything."

Not many days later visitors came in with a new
story ; the ride with the young expressman, without date or explanation. Miss Crooke crushed it.

" You may just leave that right there," she said.
" I 'm knowing to the whole of it. It was Wednesday night, in that thunderstorm, when neither you
nor I would have crossed the doorstone for a gold
mine. She went home from this house, to keep
her aunt from being scared ; and she took the only
way there was. When there ain't but one way,
and a thing 's to be done, she don't stop at it, if

it *is* over a fence. Rill Raye has got a good heart, and she's clear spunk to the backbone!'"

"Well, you do surprise me, Miss Crooke. You did n't use to talk in that way about Rill Raye. Ain't the wind kind o' got round lately?"

"Yes, Miss Upson, it has. And you need n't mind callin' me a weathercock if you'd like to, for I presume likely I am. I 've had as pertickler opportunities to judge as if I was; and I don't never insist on p'intin' east after it fairly blows west."

Putnam King heartily enjoyed the whole story. "I don't see but you 've got a plant here, for your gospel-gossip manufacture," he said. "Only all the raw material won't be of the Rill Raye sort, exactly. A girl," he added rather slowly after a pause, "who would go through fire and water for an uncomfortable old aunt whom she does n't pretend to be fond of, — or for a Miss Sally Crooke, — what would n't she do for anybody she really cared for?"

"She would go through moral fire and water. She would burn and drown, inside, for — them." Miss Haven sacrificed a bit of grammar to her hesitation in specifying gender.

Putnam King went on sketching queer outlines of faces with his aunt's stylo upon her blotting-pad for several minutes, without saying a word. Then

he remarked, nonchalantly, " If you don't introduce me to Miss Raye, aunt Elizabeth, I shall go
and call on Miss Bonable."

Miss Haven, dear, innocent old maid, had not
the least idea of what she was accomplishing ; yet
she could n't have done it better, so far, if she
had tried.

" Of course I 'll introduce you, Put," she said,
" whenever it happens so."

With all her simplicity as to live wires of occult
influence in such matters, aunt Elizabeth knew
very well that it would never do to make any obvious difficulty about this.

CHAPTER V.

"NOW YOU KNOW."

It happened so very shortly after, and without any intervention of aunt Elizabeth's. History repeated itself.

Another summer gust came up after tea one evening, when Miss Haven and Rill had settled to their now regularly established game. A whirl of wind tore in without warning through the open window, sent the light curtain draperies streaming through their looped ribbon fastenings straight into the room, enveloping dangerously for a moment the tall double-burner lamp which Rill caught quickly with both hands, averting a catastrophe. Their cards were swept to the floor, a growl of thunder rolled round the horizon, and heavy, separate drops of rain struck like shot upon the panes and thudded upon the porch roof.

Rill snatched up scarf and hat. "That's for me, again," she said. "Don't mind; I've got my parasol."

"You'd better wait," expostulated Miss Haven.

" I can't; there 's no Thrape, this time, and it would n't do twice, if there were. Thrape 's very good-looking; and he was very polite when he handed me down, with aunt Amelia standing in the doorway. She was n't impressed with simple gratitude to either of us; she 's so extremely apt to think there 's something in it, — millions of things, besides me and the right one. Good-night, dear Miss Haven. Please shut me out quick." And she slipped through the small opening which she allowed in the door, helping herself to pull it after her against the increasing drive of the slanting rain. Miss Haven had to return, a little dazed with the sudden upshot of affairs, and pick up her bézique cards.

Rill Raye stepped off the porch into the darkness, full against the broad shoulders of a man standing at the foot of the two steps, furling an umbrella. The girl started, sprang back, and the figure turned. It was too dark for them to see each other's faces; but they were not altogether in the dark, either.

" Miss Rill Raye?" asked Putnam King, at a tolerably certain venture.

" Yes; I 'm like the witches, always out in a storm. I must hurry. Good-evening, Mr. King."

" I can't say *that*, under the present dispensation of the elements;" and the umbrella went quickly up again, its owner leaning it over Rill's head, marching along the gravel walk with her to the little front gate. They were outside it and fairly moving up the street before she could finish her expostulation. The introduction was made; all in a minute they were quite well acquainted. Miss Elizabeth's simple prudence of procrastination had beautifully prepared matters.

"Is this your way? I thought my aunt told me you lived on the North Road?"

"Yes, there is a turn, presently. Brook Lane zigzags across."

Inwardly, Rill was saying to herself, "This is worse than Thrape. What shall I do with him when we get to the door?"

"Do you often go home alone, all this way, in the evenings?"

"Oh, yes; evenings are harmless in Wewachet. Sometimes, though, I take an express wagon."

"I heard of that," Mr. King said.

If he could have told her all he had thought about it since hearing, his answer would have been less succinct. He held the umbrella further over on the girl's side and well before her. Wind and rain were in their faces, but their force had momentarily abated.

"I don't think you are dividing things fairly," remarked Rill presently, in a comical little tone of aggrievement. " I have all the umbrella and you have all the rain."

" It is n't easy to divide here. We 'll do better farther along. How the street-lamps flicker ! "

" Yes ; and how far apart they are ! There are n't any at all upon the lane ; that 's why I come home by lightning — when it is n't moonlight."

" You must know the way well."

" Every step and stone of it. Mr. King," she added suddenly, half stopping, " I 'm afraid you 'll get lost going back. Do let me finish alone, now. The rain is really holding up."

" There will be light enough, and the rain is not holding up," Putnam King answered with decision.

The lightning, sheeting suddenly the cloud-hung heavens, and illuminating the tree vistas and the pathway before their feet, verified his first words.

" And besides," Rill continued, as the darkness covered them up again, " aunt Amelia always thinks I do things on purpose."

" Don't you ? " inquired Mr. King. " I do." There was a good deal of purpose in his tone at this moment.

" But she supposes some other purpose."

" That often happens with many people, I find. If we altered our course for that, there very soon would n't be any purpose left."

"Mr. King," Rill began again, "would you mind leaving me at the last corner?"

"I will mind anything you tell me that is reasonable. I will leave you as soon as I see you safe."

"Thank you."

The tone had changed between the two. Rill's bit of habitual daring and self-assertion had dropped out of her speech, and in words and accent she yielded to a new-found mastery. She took gratefully a consent where she would ordinarily have defied refusal.

The nearest corner was in full view from Miss Bonable's cottage, which stood endwise upon the street. When she let Cyrilla in Miss Bonable stood and peered into the darkness over the girl's shoulder, chin up and on tiptoe.

"What did you come on this time?" she demanded.

"These two," answered Cyrilla, showing her little feet, with an alternate lift of damp boots.

"And not a drop on head or shoulders, and this thing hasn't been opened!" Aunt Amelia passed her hand along the folded parasol. "Don't tell me!"

"I will not," answered Cyrilla, quietly, making her way in past Miss Bonable, who had still stared into the dark during her test manual of Rill's person and equipments.

A parting flash of the retreating shower lit the air suddenly and showed a man's figure standing at the turn, facing toward the cottage and lingering with a watching air.

" I might have known, — and I did know ! " said Miss Bonable, closing the door and coming back into the sitting-room. " Why can't you ever tell the honest truth ? "

" You said, 'Don't tell me;' and the honest truth is exactly what you never will believe. Aunt Amelia, *must* I be crooked because you won't let me walk plain and straight ? "

Cyrilla spoke with passion ; she contemned herself and aunt Amelia at that moment. She went off up to her own room and fastened herself in there.

Aunt Amelia sat down, angry and pale. She crossed her hands upon her lap, let her head, still erect, just touch the top of her chair-back, and her eyes fix themselves in a level line across the room upon nothing. It was an intense moment with her. She was posing all unconscious, as we often do, for the registering — in a light which photographs more than sunlight can — of an instant of vital experience. Her lips were dropped in a curve of hopeless, resentful dejection. From under her level lids shot a swerveless look of wrathful protest. She sat so for fully fifteen minutes, all alone. Then she drew in the long remonstrance of her gaze, lifted her prone hands, rested her elbows on her lap, and dropped her face into her spread fingers.

"The child I wanted to have loved so!" the words broke out through sobs. Aunt Amelia cried, and cried, and cried; and nobody knew but herself and God the deep wells of her life whence rushed those bitter tears.

The next day, when Miss Haven came in, she was as hard as ever. Rill was out.

Miss Haven hoped Miss Raye had reached home without harm.

"She was n't *wet* — to speak of," Miss Bonable answered stiffly. "I 'd more than half as lief she would have been. I don't like these tramps, evenings," she went on with a sudden, harsh frankness, "if 't *is* to your house. That was better, I thought, than being off amongst the girls, and alwers coming home caperin' with a lot. But one to herself is worse, and I believe it was that dentist man, this time. He stood at the corner while she came in alone. Why don't he come here if he wants to see her?"

That was really funny; but Miss Haven only half smiled, for pity of aunt Amelia. She would answer that question later, may be.

"Rill was alone when she left me last evening," she said, gently. "She hurried away in the storm

lest you should be anxious; and if any one joined
her afterward, I do not think it was Dr. Harriman.
I am pretty sure he was elsewhere."

Now, concerning Dr. Harriman's alibi, Miss
Haven could hardly have knowledge or proof; it
only did occur to her to associate Putnam King's
arrival some twenty minutes or more after Rill's
departure, with her possible escort home. That
Putnam had said nothing simply gave her a little
more to think of in a different or further way. "I
think her meeting any one was purely accidental,"
she said.

"She's dreadful liable to accidents," said Miss
Bonable, grimly. "And they *have* been dental,
lately," she added, strangling a smile. "As to
me, much she seemed to care about my being anxious after she got here! Miss Haven, some girls
would walk over red-hot layvey if they could only
be walked with! It isn't that I think any real
harm of Rill — so far; but it's the disposition. It
was her mother's way, and it scares me. She's in
her mother's tracks, and I know what they lead to."

The last sentences seemed to come from her lips
of themselves; her face was strained and absent;
she did not look at Miss Haven as she spoke.

"Miss Bonable! Your own sister!"

Then Miss Bonable did look round at her friend,
and met surprised, indignant, yet still pitying eyes.

"She was n't my sister," she said. "Now you
know; and you know more than anybody else in
Wewachet, except myself. Rill never knew, and
I don't mean she shall. I don't know what makes
me tell you, only you seem as if you held out your
heart to me, and what 's in mine goes into it.
You can keep it there, I suppose."

Still as grim and stiff as ever; if she had been
bidding Miss Haven go about her business, she
could not have been more uncompromising than in
uttering this confidence.

"My dear Miss Bonable!" said Elizabeth Haven. There was no less of appeal and sympathy
than of astonishment, in the exclamation. The
open heart was still held out, and, as if she could
not help it, Miss Amelia poured forth further from
her own. It was the bleeding of the wound, however; it was not with any voluntary gush of
warmth.

"He did marry my sister, first, instead of me.
We were promised; but Esther was taking and
pretty, — she could n't help that; I don't suppose
he could help it, either. I never had her coaxing
ways; I was fair-looking, and I just meant what I
said, that was all. It 's no new story; I 've read a
hundred like it; I suppose they 're happening all
round; but I *lived* mine, — that 's the difference.
When I found out what they wanted I gave her all

the things I had got ready — and been so busy
about that I had not noticed sooner. I gave her
my wedding gown; she'd rather not have had that,
but I made her. 'If you take part, you take all,'
I said. I would n't let her off. It wasn't Church
form they were married by, — it was Congrega-
tional. But I remembered one sentence in the
Episcopal that run through my head all the time
we stood before the minister: 'Who giveth this
woman to be married to this man?' I gave them
both to each other — and it was giving away all
that might ever have been soft or sweet in my life.
I've been just the hard old maid folks know here,
ever since. But there's another Amelia Bonable
that never had her life out fairly yet, and that has
got to rise up somehow in the last day and begin
again. Know each other? Folks ask that about
the next world. As if we knew the least bit what
to look for half the time! It'll generally be somebody else, I guess; if we're sure of ourselves, it's
as much as we shall be!"

Miss Bonable was thinking aloud some of the
thoughts that had filled and chafed her silent soli-
tudes. Miss Haven did not interrupt her.

"Sometimes I think her conscience broke her
heart when she saw how altered I was, and how I
stayed altered. She only lived two years. And
then Marcus Raye was ashamed and afraid to come

back to me, even like a brother. He kept off, and there was no word for me to say; and, in a year after, he married that Loraine Braitway. He must have been wild; it was a kind of making away with himself. Her name was up then, for her flirtings and jiltings; and afterwards it was worse, — as bad as things can be with a woman. She went off, out West somewhere, — nobody knows. And he turned straight the other way and went to Australia. Before he went he came to me, — they'd lived on in Maplefield, down East, where all the first of it happened, and I'd come here, where uncle Bonable's folks used to live. Nobody in Wewachet knew, when he left the child here, that it wasn't my sister's; so I've held my tongue and given her the advantage. She's got a good deal of Mark in her, but the thought of the mother keeps me on the tenterhooks."

" Rill does n't know you; and you do not trust her." Miss Haven did not stop to put in words of sympathy or admiration; she passed without delay to the point that vitally concerned the two.

"That's it; and that is how it has to be. I'm glad I've told you; I'm glad one person understands, and that it's you. It's a comfort to have somebody know the other of me. I used to be *Amy* — when I was alive. You would n't think so now."

Miss Haven leaned toward her, took her hand
and kissed her. "My dear Miss Amy!" she said.
Then the hard face quivered, a change ran over
it, the straightened cheeks took softer curves, and
hot tears — a baptism of tenderness — ran over
them.

"I thank you for letting me see your hidden,
beautiful self," Miss Haven told her, still keeping
the poor, feverish hand that moved restlessly in her
kindly clasp.

"You won't" — Miss Bonable began, and then
lifting her eyes to her friend's, "No, I'll not ask
you," she said. "You don't hear for curiosity, and
you won't tell for talk!"

"No," said Miss Haven. "You have trusted
me, and I will be faithful; but to be faithful,
might be, some time, to speak. More harm is done
sometimes by keeping secret than by repeating.
And there is one thing I shall take my first chance,
and every chance, to say. There is a noble woman
among these Wewachet people, of whom they do
not know the half. They shall know that they do
not know. I like to stimulate interest in the right
direction; I like to set the best to finding out the
other best."

"Don't say anything to Rill."

"I shall say a great many things to Rill. She
shall not be cheated of her duty and her gratitude.

But I shall bide my time, and you need not be afraid."

Somehow, when Miss Haven left her, Miss Bonable felt as if she had only once more told her story to the Lord, and got a word from Him she had not had before.   She was not afraid to leave it so.

CHAPTER VI.

THERE is more than one thread to the simplest yarn. It is time to show a little of Dr. Harriman's relations with our small chronicle, and of how they were already affecting that gentleman. It is as true of a man as of a woman, that with some really fine points of character there may undeniably co-exist some frivolities. Dr. Harriman knew very well that he was handsome and noticeable in many ways, and that his coming into any new scene or neighborhood was apt to make a certain sensation. He was aware that young feminine eyes glanced — or more than glanced — at him with a favoring interest, and that the possibilities of life suggested themselves more or less dimly or positively, with more or less of delicious wonder and speculation, to the youthful feminine mind at his approach. He knew that the set of his Sunday coat across his shapely shoulders was an august and sacred thing in the vision of these girls, whose own little mysteries of fold and ribbon and trinket were managed in conscious counterpart, and meant to be sweetly, if not as imposingly, impressive in their turn. And Dr. Harriman was not indifferent to the pleasure of being universally and instantly welcome, or to the fact that words from his lips, or little courtesies of course at his hands, had the delicate charm aimed at by Sam Weller in his love letters. He measured words and attentions judiciously, for the most part, reserving the more for the time and person that should find him in sober earnest to give. He did not intend to give yet awhile ; he did not mean to marry until he had thoroughly and deliberately arranged for the comfort of marriage.

It is perhaps a hazardous matter for the feminine pen to meddle with, — the inward working of little weaknesses and possible noblenesses in masculine character ; but the meanderings of motive and impulse in the human heart are always human, and it may be that the man or woman nature is on either side as a key to the bolt which bars the secrecies of the other. Coquetry in a woman is the pleasure of assurance that she can cause by her attraction the seeking and asking side of creation to come to her feet with wish and plea ; some women travel the whole round of life as the moon does the firmament, drawing a tide after her which — Heaven knows what good it does her — must simply ebb itself back at its unchanged, hopeless distance of two hundred and forty thousand miles. In a man, this self-pleasure is the complacency one might fancy in the sturdier substance of the earth-orb, which betrays no visible pulse or movement, but which holds the moon fast in her orbit at the near but maiden limit which she must not pass. To leave the insufficient metaphor, some women delight in little experimental evidences of what they might receive if they would take it ; some men in the sense of 'power to make serious claim if they would. It is fine to think one may command possession ; perhaps it is yet finer to feel that one can confer sublimely, when one's mind shall be quite made up to do so. On either side there may be, with all preliminary small vanity, material for good, honest loving and living, when the lighter prelude has been played out. Meantime there remain the hazards of the edge tools and the fire.

Dr. Robert Harriman was not a silly trifler ; he was in earnest with his life ; but he was capable of a certain surface amusement while the earnest waited. In his case it had to wait, or he thought so ; he was helping a younger brother through college, and he had sustained the expense of a sister's wedding outfit. His mother needed no direct help from him, but he saved her these demands which would have been too **heavy** for her. If others

came, of sickness or loss, he must stand ready.   He
could not marry yet awhile.   But that the sublime
conferring was in his hand he was well reminded
by such girls as Connie Norris; and their open
wiles   and   candid   beguilements   warranted,   he
thought, a certain degree of tolerance, or even innocently " tentative " response.   With Cyrilla Raye
it was different.   Evidently, here he must make
approach if he desired it; evidently, also, it would
have to be with decided and significant endeavor.

She had kept her resolve to know nothing of
him after that heroic introduction, until an every-
day presentation should take place in some inevitable manner.   Her dignity was reinforced by loy-
alty.   She had recognized Connie's preëmption of
privilege ; with severity of honor she renounced interference with what had been assumed in the confidence of immature, effusive friendship.

She met Dr. Harriman several times before anybody thought of the due formalities ; the tittle-
tattle about her adventure had of course put the
matter in inference as a thing accomplished.   People were rather conjecturing how the acquaintance
would go on; wondering at the mutual aloofness.
The two themselves were quietly curious as to
whether any acquaintance would ever be begun.

When at length one day, thrown together in a
call at the same house, the friend who received

them, embarrassed at their non-recognition, said questioningly, " Dr. Harriman — Miss Raye, you know Dr. Harriman ? " Rill answered from a remote height, with a carefully measured inclination of her little head, " Certainly; I know who Dr. Harriman is ; but we are not acquainted — yet ! "

" I thank you for that last little word, Miss Raye ; I hope it means that you will not refuse me the privilege any longer? " and the doctor, who had already risen from his chair, made Rill the most charming bow, deferent, not emphasized, and bent full upon her, with a certain admiring respect, the eyes which all the young womanhood of Wewachet voted " splendid," and which the Irish maid at the Norrises was known to have declared were " jist the coaxinest two she iver seen wid a man."

Miss Raye bowed, and smiled a little in return ; then made some inconsequential remark such as hyphenizes conversation when it might otherwise fall apart too significantly into fragments. If she had been the most practiced woman of the world, she could not have done it better than from her quick, girlish instinct. Dr. Harriman was freshly piqued to peculiar interest.

Every time they met, it was just so. Whatever Rill Raye might be with other people, with Dr.

Harriman she was provoking, elusive, cool; she
was pointedly out of the lists; she left him to
Connie and Sue and the rest of them, who were
ready to tear him into little bits — of social appropriation — and each run off with a piece, like
chickens with a big, tough, tempting morsel.

Miss Haven perceived what she thought the
girl's judicious dignity, based upon a real indiffer-
ence ; and so she was not afraid when the two met
sometimes in her library. She liked them both; if
they came to understand and like each other better, it would not trouble her sense of responsibility. Since her talk with Miss Bonable, it had
more than once occurred to her that a safe, right
marriage for Cyrilla would be the only solving of
the problem of their troubled, mutually mistaking
lives. And she knew that Miss Bonable's only
prejudice against the doctor lay in her idea of the
present status of his acquaintance with her niece.
This once properly established, above-board, — possibly even transferred to Miss Amelia's own au-
spices at the cottage, as she had with such naive
inconsistency demanded why not, — there need be
no hindrance to whatever might truly and happily
come of it.

Miss Haven's thoughts did not meddle further;
she was no deliberate matchmaker. Whether or
not the circumstance that neither Putnam King

nor Cyrilla had mentioned to her the little occurrence of their walk in the rain together, though
they also had now met on a footing of regular acquaintance under her own countenance, worked in
some recondite fashion with her to cause this leaning toward the chance of liking between Dr. Harriman and Rill as the course that the providence
for Rill might take, she certainly would have
leaned away from any suggestion arising in this
other quarter. It was too soon for Putnam King
to think of such matters. He had to take a man's
place in the world before he could ask a wife to
his side. Not that money, or the lack of it, would
be a difficulty; half the property of a bachelor
uncle had come to him, depriving him of the spur
of need. This was a loss to his life, aunt Elizabeth felt, which must be replaced by some other
energy before he could fairly or wisely accept the
things of life that are better after some earning
and striving. He was simply aside from any calculation of hers in this sort; and undoubtedly also
her desire for the very best for him in every sort
would have led her instinctively to shrink in his
behalf from decision that might be premature,
while opportunities and comparison were yet im-
perfect. She would not choose a silk gown for
herself from the very first piece; there might be a
better. Dr. Harriman could do his own choosing.

It is difficult for mothers and aunts to understand that their own boys can.

Meanwhile, affairs were not very much complicated. The two young men had thus far rarely happened to meet at Miss Haven's.

CHAPTER VII.

WHEAT-SEED AND TARE-SEED.

Miss Norris had arranged to take lessons in china painting in town during school vacation. She was still, at eighteen, a pupil in one of the fine seminaries for girls at the West Bay.

Dr. Harriman had a regular day for some city business connected with his profession ; he always went into town on Saturdays.

Cornelia Norris found Tuesday and Saturday to be the only days she could appoint with her teacher for her china work.

So one of the later Saturday afternoon trains brought these two among other constant passengers to Wewachet, almost invariably. It was almost invariable, I mean, that they found themselves on the same train ; though the trips were figured thickly along the time-table toward the end of the day, occurring every hour until after six, when there was a gap until 8.30.

Connie's lesson was over at four ; but of course there were often errands, afterward. Very fre-

quently a train slipped off without her, when she
had to buy a ticket at the last minute, or sat near
the sashed opening into the entrance hall, en-
grossed with a new paper-covered volume bought at
the news-stand. Once in a while something had
been forgotten, or a parcel did not arrive; and she
turned her back on train and station, to go up-
town again before the next scheduled departure.
Through all these vicissitudes and uncertainties —
one must use prepositions advisedly — it rarely
happened that our two friends made the Saturday
return separately. And since, in a common car,
one must have a seatmate, what more natural than
that they should easily drift together?

I do not think Dr. Harriman can be blamed,
exactly; it was really almost inevitable for him.
The nicety with which movements, observations,
instinctive perceptions and calculations can be
made, involving the right coincidences at risk of
the utterly wrong ones from any least failure, is
something to wonder at applaudingly, and to recognize as the working of occult power, at once
surer and more delicate than harsh mathematics,
and, so, perhaps, more particularly adapted to feminine engineering. Connie Norris scarcely ever
came out at a loss; the wish of Dr. Harriman, if
he had one, like the heart of the husband in the
Proverbs of Solomon, might safely trust in her;

if he now and then played to the same purpose by
some slight hint or watchfulness, some lingering
or hastening on his own part ; if it was a pleasant
bit of excitement to him to find the pretty figure
and the bright, gladdening face at a sure point for
being found ; to check his steps for the expected
greeting, and then have hers take up, as of course,
their light accompaniment alongside, as with the
stream of outgoing passengers they went through
the great gates to the train-house and the track
platform together ; or to discover her already
seated with a vacant place beside her, when he
came half expectantly and fully expected, along
the car-aisle just three minutes, perhaps, after he
had stopped at the news-counter, and she had
scudded innocently on, observant, apparently, of
nothing but the big hands of the clock over the
gateway ; to be shown, as they journeyed, her last
lovely plaque, or exquisite quaint jug, just brought
safe from the firing ; if all this was put frankly
and cheerily in his way, why not accept it frankly
and cheerily also, *en bon camaraderie?* None
the less, perhaps, he perceived her, as he had at
first, to be a " simpleton ; " but a simpleton can
be very honestly bewitching ; the openness and
the honesty took away something of the triviality,
and abated the contempt. He found it a pas-
time to be with her ; it was also a study of character, as far as the character went.

At the same time that all this was going on, there was an interest of precisely opposite sort developing in Dr. Harriman's mind toward Cyrilla Raye; an interest piqued by reserve and difficulty and the complexities of a higher individuality. Cyrilla puzzled him; and a man will go further out of his way to solve a problem than he will to read a plainly advertised fact.

I will not vouch for it that Cyrilla did not perceive, with a new demureness shielding her discovery, that she had stumbled, through whim, upon a more effective rôle than all her gay abandon had furnished her with before; or that a certain triumph did not turn her first honest, withdrawing pride into something of a fresh and fascinating experiment.

Almost to her own bewilderment, Rill Raye was slipping into a new position in Wewachet, and began to feel it in the air about her. " People will talk," she had said once to Miss Haven's friendly monitions of prudence, " and after they 've once begun, you can't change the keynote you 've given them. They expect something startling from me; if I were as tame as an old house-cat for ten years, it would n't make any difference, there would n't be anything worth mentioning in that; they 'd either invent something, or go back to the last piece of wildness in my infancy. I shall have to finish up as I 've set out, or disappoint the world."

Miss Haven, with good reason, thought otherwise.

In fact, a different sort of strikingness in Rill's performances had begun to appear. Some old stories got a new moral to them, and started on a fresh run. Nobody knew how it was found out, but a supplement had here and there been put to fragmentary narrations which both rounded out and pointed them, making them good for another circulation.

"That Miss Raye is a pretty girl; but she makes mistakes," said one lady to another at a social gathering where Rill was prominent. " Was n't there some sauciness of hers at Lill Upson's when three or four partners came to her at once for the reel ? "

" Oh, yes, that 's an old story. She flirted her fan in their faces, told them there were too many of them, and she would n't dance at all; and then marched off, leaving them *plantés la.* Afterward, for oddity and fun, she got up and danced on the men's side, with a girl partner."

" But that was n't all of it," said a third person standing by. "Mollie Wythe had been sitting out, forgetting, in her meek little way, that there was anything possible for her to do but to look on and admire Rill Raye and the rest. Plain, awkward little thing, she had got used to it. Rill suddenly took in the injustice of it, when all those boys stood round her, asking at once, and sticking out their elbows; she fairly pushed John Lownes's down. ' It's a shame of you, all coming for one girl,' she said. ' Why don't you divide round?' and she turned her back, and walked up to Mollie. ' Dance this with me,' she said. ' I 'll be gentleman. They 're scarce here to-night.' And off they went, and Mollie had her good time of the evening. Rill never thought of the men's line till she got there, except to show them what a gentleman should do, as she said."

" It made a new conspicuousness for her though; she had her fun out of it; marching them all after her up and down the room, like captives at a Roman show," said the lady who had told the tale.

"That was how it appeared, and was, as far as it went. But it was n't the best of it, or what she did it for. There 's something in Rill Raye besides audacity."

"I wish there were n't that, then," returned the matron who had spoken first of all; but her tone relented. "It is n't the right style, you know; somebody ought to tell her not to have too good a time."

The three speakers — Mrs. Rextell, Mrs. Vance,

and Mrs. Sholto — were of the high ladyhood of Wewachet.

It was not long after this that Mrs. Rextell made one of her biennial calls upon Miss Bonable, and followed it by cards for that lady and her niece to her large garden-party.

"No, indeed," Miss Bonable had said to Miss Haven, who spoke of it, taking acceptance for granted. "It's her hash party. She's had little private companies all summer. Why did n't she ask me to any of them, I wonder?"

"For the same reason, I suppose, that she did not ask me. I had not any little private rights."

"Poh! Everybody knows you can go any-where."

"I don't admit the contrary of you."

Miss Bonable saw that she had admitted it, and retreated into momentary silence.

"If you do not go, let me take Cyrilla."

Miss Bonable opened her eyes wide. "*Take* Cyrilla!" she ejaculated. "It's rather late in the day to begin on that plan. She has taken herself — wherever she could get — so far."

"May be that has been a mistake. I should like to have her with me?" The interrogative was a petition.

"*I* can't hinder," said Miss Bonable, concisely.

So it was under Miss Haven's unimpeachable

wing that Rill Raye went, chaperoned for the first
occasion in her life, to Mrs. Rextell's.

"Don't have too good a time, dear," said Miss
Haven, with gentlest significance, as they drove up
the long, sweeping approach, on either side of
which, under the splendid groups of tall trees, the
guests, in dainty array, were already scattering
about upon the green velvet of the closely mown
grass. Had Mrs. Rextell ever suggested the
kindly hypothesis to Miss Elizabeth, or had Miss
Elizabeth herself originally started it on its way —
that the only trouble with Rill Raye was that she
had too good a time, too undisguisedly? I think it
had been a bit of the gospel gossip.

Miss Haven would have had her hands full to-
day, if she thought to scatter good seed as fast as
the evil one would cast the tares. Everything was
astir and afloat, from the minute Dr. Harriman
and Connie Norris walked up the lawn, as they
did a few minutes after Miss Haven and Cyrilla
had arrived ; and certain comments reached Mrs.
Rextell's ears which inclined her to regret, notwithstanding the comprehensive intent of her neighborhood gathering — her hash party — that these two
should be there together. They had met just below the gates ; these little fortuitous circumstances
had fallen into a law of recurrence that seemed to
work now of itself, really without premeditation ;

to the doctor it was beginning to present a difficulty; it was becoming too invariable; yet every
time he fell for the moment into the pleasant
snare.

"*Do* you see? *Did* you notice?" passed from
lip to lip among certain of the observers; and one
connected tale was set forth with fresh gusto by a
brisk little lady with an animated bunch of tall
rudbeckias in her hat, that bobbed and danced
from left to right and up and down, in the eager
motion of the wearer, as she addressed her speech
and nodded its emphasis and tossed its sneer;
and from her it traveled till the lady of the manor
listened, displeased, to the slighter remarks con-
veying the impression of the story into which it
condensed itself in the rendering of the thorough-
bred.

"*Actually*, she got off the train within half a
minute of its starting. I put my head out of the
window and saw the whole. She met him at the
gate. There was some pretense or other, as usual;
I suppose he told her there was n't time; and then
they both hurried down the platform. But the
bell rang, and we slipped off, just as they came
alongside the last car. *He* could have got on, but
he would n't let her, and he could n't leave her;
so there they were, and no train for two hours and
a half — and *evening!*"

"So they went back, and sat down, and looked at decorated plates, I suppose, instead of going home to their suppers?"

"My *dear!* waste opportunities like that — and go hungry? No, indeed! They went up town, and had tea at Bever's, and walked about afterward till train time; she told of it herself, as a great lark. I wonder they did n't stay in and go to the theatre. Perhaps they will, next time."

And it may as well be mentioned here that the next time the story was told, or took a fresh departure, the theatre addition was put on as an assertion; and that so in the end it worked its way round, till Dr. Harriman heard it, to his intense annoyance and disgust; the more that he perceived he had really been going too far, and that he had only himself to thank for whatever misconstruction might accrue.

That there was a glaring inconsistency between these escapades and the quieter significance of the visits at Crooke Corner, aggravated both the young doctor's self-dissatisfaction and his difficulties with Cyrilla Raye.

Meantime, on the Rextell lawn to-day, the last-named young lady was superbly inaccessible.

CHAPTER VIII.

THE POND LILY ROOM.

"You're on a new tack, Rill," said Connie Norris, coming up to her after Rill had a third time evaded a prolonged interview with the doctor, whose sudden "dividing of himself round" by no means pleased Miss Connie. "And you are taking all the wind out of other people's sails."

"I haven't set any sails," said Rill, with the brief gravity so new and so particularly becoming to her.

"I wish you would, then," said Connie, frowning. "It would be fairer than the way you're doing now."

Rill flashed a look at her without speaking.

Just then Dr. Harriman appeared once more, escorting Miss Haven. "There is tea down there, under the beeches," he said. "Would you like to go for some, or shall I bring it to you here?" He addressed the three ladies, as he paused with Miss Elizabeth.

"We will go down, I think," said Miss Elizabeth. "There is more there than tea. That, one can take at home, you know. We came here to enjoy people."

Rill had a high color, and her eyes burned yet with the light that had made Connie's blink. She took Miss Haven's arm with a little private grip of determination, and there was nothing left for Dr. Harriman but to follow with Cornelia.

Another moving group brushed by. The breeze brought back some semi-detached words spoken just after it had passed.

" Engaged ? "

" Or ought to be."

Rill and Miss Haven both heard it. Each wondered silently whether the pulse of sound had reached back to the other two.

Rill's head was an inch or two higher as she walked on. She hurried Miss Haven, drawing her forcibly forward, and putting an increasing distance between the other couple and themselves. This was quite practicable, for Connie Norris did not hurry Dr. Harriman at all. She stopped him, indeed, just beyond the outskirt of the groups about the table.

" Miss Haven," said Cyrilla, in a quick, intense way, " Connie is an awful goose. But they are talking hatefully about her. Can't you hush it up ? "

Around one of the tables, where the eldest Miss
Rextell was dispensing chocolate, had gathered an
admiring bevy of friends, in the midst of whom
she sat, a stately beauty with dark hair distractingly
knotted high upon the graceful head, close against
which shone a single aster-like flower of luminous
pale violet, color of the ethereal heart-flame of the
diamond, born of highest light. She served with
dainty fingers the delicious beverage topped with
white foam of cream on every cup, and with dazzle
of smile gave right and left at the same time the
light-whipped cream of talk, without which, at such
moments, conversation would seem too seriously
nutritive.

As Miss Haven and Cyrilla came up, some one
who had finished her chocolate was turning the
empty cup about with little airs of apprehensive
ecstasy, exclaiming with soft, well-trained vehe-
mence at the rare coloring and design of the frail
bit of porcelain.

" And you have these things out *here !* " she said.
" How do you *dare ?* What are your servants
made of ? Anything corresponding to Dresden in
comparison with Delft ? "

" Hardly," said Miss Rextell, with the smile that
was like a summer electric flash, soft and swift,
that one watches eagerly for, because it is never
fixed for the merest space of a breath. " But now

that people can all paint their own teacups, and everything can be copied, one does n't seem to care so anxiously — do you think? "

This was Miss Haven's chance.

"Miss Norris paints beautifully. Did you ever see any of her work? " she asked.

The momentary drop of silence befell that marks some otherwise imperceptible little chasm to be leaped.

Some one claimed Miss Rextell's official attention. Then the lady next Miss Haven, not to slight Miss Haven herself, responded with a touch of remoteness, —

"Miss Norris? I don't think I have. Does she paint for sale? "

"Partly," returned Miss Haven, serenely. "Not from need, of course; but she makes her lessons independent, and she has other pleasant little things in her power, you know. I could tell you better if she were not close by," she added, rapidly, in a lowered voice. "But it was very nice of her, paying a livery bill for that poor little sick dressmaker of hers, for a fortnight's rides. And the things she does must simply be an exquisite pleasure to do."

"Ah, indeed? " the same lady returned, with the same far-offness.

There was still a little chasm. The name of Miss Norris had been too recently quoted in a dif-

ferent connection ; and there was Dr. Harriman,
bringing her at this moment among them for her
tea.

. Miss Rextell leaped the gulf. It was the prettiest leap possible. She left her chair, her soft white
draperies making a gracious light about her, and
moved gently through the way that was parted for
her, out upon the open lawn.

"Good evening, Miss Norris," she said to her
guest. "I had not seen you before. Will you
have chocolate ? Or, there is tea close by. Dr.
Harriman, please to find what Miss Norris likes.
The chocolate is at my table." And with one of
her bewildering smiles, and a word about the lovely
weather, and that she was so glad there could be
so many here, she glided back again.

"Here is a place by me, Miss Haven. Will you
have more sugar ? One of these little cocoanut
puffs ?—I 'm glad you told that nice thing of Miss
Norris," she said, in a quiet, friendly tone. "There
is always more than one story to know. Don't
you think, Miss Haven," she went on, in a clear,
sweet, incisive voice, "that, after all, the chief difference between people is their different way of
doing the same things ? "

All her immediate circle heard the words, and a
counter wave to the creep of the hostile motion in
these Wewachet waters was set stirring around

Cornelia Norris. The drift of it touched her at once; she found herself more in the pleasant current. An edge opened where she stood, and she was taken in by some gentle, casual recognitions, when she might have remained quite outside, without having any positive rudeness to complain of.

When Miss Haven had finished her chocolate, she rose and quietly made her way again toward her escort.

"Dr. Harriman," she said, "will you be kind enough to help me find Mrs. Rextell?" and taking his offered arm, she walked away up the lawn with him.

She had effected a modification and change among the elements toward a more beneficent solution. But, blessed busybody that she was, she had not yet done for the day. She meant that this afternoon, which threatened to be the turning-point for ill, socially, in a heedless young girl's life, should revert to quite an opposite accomplishment.

Joining Mrs. Rextell, she slipped into conversation with her, leaving Dr. Harriman to such liberty as he might like to take. So, presently, for a brief chance, the two ladies were left apart a little.

"Dear Mrs. Rextell," said Miss Haven then, "your daughter Margaret has just done such a sweet and gracious thing." And she told her the how and the why. "I wish — I think — you will do another."

" In what fashion ? "

" Your own fashion ; you will know how. It
will make such a difference. There was a cloud
coming up for that young girl."

" I am glad Margaret behaved just so. But" —
and the lady's fair dignity, that was shy, even in its
own purity, took a touch of regretful shrinking.
" I don't like girls to get under a cloud," she said.

" Beam out upon her, please ! Drive the cloud
away — for this time at least. You can."

At the moment, the two young girls approached
up the slope, pausing a little way off when they
saw Miss Haven engaged with Mrs. Rextell.

" How pretty she is ! " said Mrs. Rextell, honestly. " But I like the other one's face better."

" Yes ; they are both pretty girls. And I am
very fond of Cyrilla Raye."

Mrs. Rextell moved forward.

" Miss Norris," she said, — and there were people enough about to see and hear and be surprised,
among them the very lady of the rudbeckias, who
had hovered within speaking distance of Mrs. Rextell and her changing coterie for half an hour, without apparent reason or result, — " Miss Norris, I
hear you are fond of art, and do pretty things in
color yourself. Will you come into the house with
me ? I should like to show you something. Miss
Raye, you will come too, won't you ? "

And, with that way a lady can have of being occupied with just the persons and the errand she
chooses, Mrs. Rextell, laying her hand on Miss Haven's arm, led the little party indoors.

It was a distinguishment. It left people turning
their heads, and wondering quietly. Dr. Harriman
himself noticed, and was impressed.

Upstairs, through Mrs. Rextell's own beautiful
room, out into a corridor beyond, which connected
with a new wing lately added to the mansion, with
a pretty staircase coming up from another side,
they passed to a suite of dainty, small apartments
in a row, all fronting upon the lawn. Doors, easily
sliding, but as easily closed to complete separation,
linked and divided them within.

" I want to show you my pond lily room," the
hostess said, walking on to the door from the gallery in the farther end and throwing it open.
" We shall hardly have time for the others now;
but I would like you to see this. It is where I put
my very dearest, sweetest young girl friends when
they come to me. I made it for them. There are
not many to whom I give it. They are of the pond
lily nature themselves. I have a wild rose room beside; and a marigold chamber, and a little fernery,
where my older visitors who want real rest and in-
visibility, can stay. But this " — and she stood
aside, and let the lovely surprise speak for itself.

Exquisite shades of gray and green made up the
tone of color in the charming apartment.

The carpet was of a cool, soft water-gray, with
white rugs laid about upon it; its border was a
deep, dull green. Walls were covered with like
tints, the frieze and dado giving the repeat of restful green, broken and characterized in the dado by
decoration of tall, swaying reeds and grasses.

In chosen places — over the low bed-head, which
had no canopy, and at one side above the dressing-
table, and again by the window, knotted above the
wainscot and continued down upon it in beautiful
drops and tassels, were twisted stems and buds and
blossoms of the water-lily, painted by an artist's
hand. There was embroidery of lilies on the
folded down coverlet of dark green silk.

But upon and about a large oval table with gray
marble slab was the masterpiece of loveliness, —
the toilet array all daintily set forth. The porcelain basin — broad and deep, like a veritable little
lake — was of pale gray in ground color, upon
which wandered olive stems and dark green pads,
while leaning up against and over the brim were
buds and blossoms that one might almost fancy
would be astir and afloat when the bowl should be
filled with water. The quaint, round-swelling. close-
throated jug held clusters falling out from stems
that seemed thrust within, and dropped the fair,

white heads upon the great curving side, two or three winding the handle with loose turns and falling with their budded tips behind. A smaller pitcher had just one light knot looped round it, the stem ends curling away on one side and two golden-hearted open blooms hanging over upon the other. Beneath the table a luxurious foot bath completed the appliances, about whose oval the flowers and leaves and coiling stems were actually heaped, so that it would seem like dipping in beneath their cool, sweet shelter to find the pool they hid.

All the hangings of the room were in green and white, — dusky green with olive lights, and pure, creamy, ivory fairness. Dressing-table held its own exquisite service of porcelain and ivory, upon which here and there some echo of the same design was repeated. Over all the soft, faint blue tinting of the ceiling closed, like distant sky.

Cornelia Norris was in a real ecstasy. The art — the perfection of the execution — excited her with delight. She moved from one thing to another, hanging over each, or glancing up and down at answering touches of beauty, with an eager taking in of the charm of the purpose and the marvelous skill of the carrying out. Rill Raye stood by, very quiet, in the midst of it all. Mrs. Rextell turned to her. " You like it ? "

There were tears in the girl's eyes.

" I think," said Rill, " that if it were not quite a pond lily nature, to be put in here would almost make it so."

" That is the sweetest thing anybody has ever said of it yet! " said Mrs. Rextell. She laid her hand upon Rill's shoulder with a friendly, caressing touch.

" Oh, see this bud, Rill! How the pink blushes through the olive! It is just celestial to see color laid on so! "

" One thinks of the laying on ; the other feels the heart of the meaning. I like your girl best," said Mrs. Rextell to Miss Haven as they went down-stairs.

CHAPTER IX

CONNIE NORRIS was beginning to find her coincidences becoming less felicitous. Her story all at
once was running bare of occurrence.

Dr. Harriman was growing indifferent, or cautious, she could not tell which; he was certainly a
little queer. He had gone into another car, one day
when they had taken the same train to the city.
She had been in the file of passengers with him at
the steps; he had seen her and bowed; then he
had gone across the platform to the rear carriage,
and when she had paused, glancing hesitatingly
that way herself, and had half followed, he had
turned, and said politely, "This is the smoker, Miss
Connie," and disappeared over the threshold.

Miss Haven had been very disagreeable one day.
" Old Meddleprate," Connie in her inward wrath
had called her, then and afterward. Miss Haven
had meddled, in the only way consonant with her
principles, by going straight to the person concerned
with her comment.

"Miss Connie, my dear," she had said, "an old woman sees things sometimes that a young one does not. We hear things, too. I am going to say frankly to you what I would resent for you, if I heard your affairs impertinently discussed. Don't you think it would be wise, perhaps, to change your day for going to town? People will remark when an attractive young girl receives continued attentions, — and sometimes the remarks are a little unkind."

Connie had tossed her head, and said she did n't see that she could help it. People went in the cars every day, and her days with Miss Tintwell could not be managed differently.

When Dr. Harriman took coldly to the smoker, or cruelly read his evening paper, she wondered if "Old Meddleprate" had been frank with him also.

Somebody had been frank with Dr. Harriman, but it had not been Miss Haven. Indeed, since that word "Engaged?" which had reached his ear with its significance, he had begun to be a little frank with himself, and to shape his behavior accordingly. But another word had been spoken, with a directness of which perhaps only one person in Wewachet was exactly capable.

Rill Raye was really fond of Connie Norris, though she did call her an awful goose. She felt herself to blame in the matter of Dr. Harriman,

that she had helped on that first wild escapade
which had begun the acquaintance; and a certain
little guiltiness troubled her, innocent of design as
she knew herself to be, in the perception that what
Connie called "sailing on a new tack" was drawing Dr. Harriman toward herself with some interest more evident than was manifest in all the light
devotedness which Connie complained was inter-
fered with.

Rill was moved by a threefold indignation — or
impatience; with Connie, with the doctor, and herself. So one day when she came into the library
at the Point, and, passing through the reading-room,
saw Connie and Dr. Harriman on opposite sides of
the same pamphlet-strewn table, she went on to the
desk without salutation, and was returning in the
same manner, her head a little higher than was
quite necessary, when the librarian spoke her name
with a recall.

"The book you asked for has just been brought
in, Miss Raye," she said, as Rill returned to the
upper end of the room; and in the little delay of
transfer and delivery, Rill caught involuntarily a
side glimpse of a transaction which sent her chin
up a slight lift higher.

Connie had written something on a slip of paper
and pushed it across upon a Saturday Review to
the doctor. The gentleman read, and answered

verbally, in the low tone and few words to which the rules restricted conversation. Connie pulled back the book and crumpled the paper. At a table close by, Rill saw glances and smiles and eyebrow-creeps exchanged, and the expression of her own face became unmistakable.

As she went out and drew the door behind her, she was conscious of a movement, and of a step following; a moment after, Dr. Harriman was beside her on the street. He gave her a pleasant greeting. Rill turned and flashed that strong expression full upon him. " Don't you know, Dr. Harriman," she said, in her clear, unflinching way, " that you are making Connie Norris talked about ? "

" Am I ? " He was too much of a gentleman to say more; but in the inflection of the two words there was, with unaffronted deference to herself, a slight underquery — " Is it all my fault ? "

" You are an honest friend, Miss Raye," he said, " and a brave one ; but is n't there sure to be talk in Wewachet, whatever one does — or does not do ? "

" It must needs be that offenses come, I suppose," Rill said to that, succinctly ; and left him to supply the remainder of the quotation for himself.

" I should be sorry to have you think ill of me,

Miss Raye," said Dr. Harriman, when they had walked again a few steps further in silence.

"The hardest thing is to have to think ill of one's self," said Rill gravely; "that is terrible."

She spoke almost impersonally; whether in caution, or admonition, or any exaggerated consciousness, lay her meaning, Dr. Harriman could hardly judge.

"I think you cannot possibly know much of what that would be," he said.

Rill looked up at him suddenly, as if out of momentary abstraction. "You cannot know anything about that," she answered him. And then she turned to leave him. "I have an errand for my aunt," she said, at the threshold of a shop door. "Good afternoon, Dr. Harriman."

It was after this that Dr. Harriman began to be queer and uncertain about his railway arrangements, and to take to evening papers and the smoker.

Miss Haven had not stopped with the disagreeable, however. She had been kind as well as frank with Cornelia Norris. She had made her welcome as a visitor to herself; and Connie, notwithstanding her resentment and her epithets, had accepted the sweet with the bitter, and availed herself of what she could get.

Miss Haven began to have quiet little afternoon

teas. On certain days, when her friends came in,
the silver teakettle was found upon her table, with
baskets of delicate cakes; and people lingered in
pleasant pairs and knots until sometimes the not
very large room was full. But somehow it was
never a "hash party;" the little word of being
usually at home on these days was only spoken to
a few, and they were mostly young people whom
Miss Haven attracted about her, and among whom
was a promotion of pleasant, informal intercourse
that made them all really better acquainted, under
such conditions of open limit as called for neither
surveillance nor criticism. Miss Haven disliked
very much a set form of matronizing; it was only
required, she thought, when most really useless, or
as an endorsing of what had better not be en-
dorsed. She thought more homelike social opportunities ought to be arranged, and that much of
what is called "going into society" was a mere
hindering bewilderment, and no sociality at all.

Perhaps the immediate reminding motive of all
this was a generous interest for Dr. Harriman and
Connie. If there must be observation and talk
of them, let it be brought here, under her countenance; it should be diverted, at any rate, from
the railway trains. If it meant anything more than
flirtation, let it have its fair, suitable chance, where
the meaning might be apparent and responsible.

Miss Haven was bent upon no one thing so much as that all things should be exactly right and true for every one. Possibly the good lady had not reckoned on the extension of Putnam King's opportunities; her "afternoons" were not the same on which he had ordinarily come; but the young man's arrangements proved very flexible, and he not only contrived to time himself with these new privileges, but fell into the way of frequent unexpected arrivals, which were rapidly establishing themselves into a rule of exceptions.

Aunt Elizabeth, however, was no believer in manœuvre or control, to advance or repress. With her own gentle presence and oversight, she ventured to let things take their immediate unembarrassed course. The two young men were beginning to know each other better, and she liked this. If Putnam King were gravitating toward another special attraction, it was with no nonsense of trivial demonstration, but with a certain manly sobriety that now and then surprised her with its contrast to his ordinary gay, free, almost boyish fashions of speech and bearing. And it pleased her to see how the pond lily beauty grew in the sweet reserves of Rill Raye, and how the new, fair dignity enfolded the girl with its garment of grace. The elder lady looked upon her with a sense of motherly adoption which became stronger day by day, and began insensibly, I think, to offset the force of that first fixed postulate of hers, that Putnam King had so much in his own life to shape, and so much other life to see, before he could be drawn by any charm whatever toward positive thought of his future serious relations.

Dr. Harriman found in the safe limitations of the intercourse now opened a happy retreat into friendly courtesy from more express and compromising assiduities. But Miss Connie Norris was not so satisfied, as we have seen. She must have conspicuous attendance. She delighted in events, adventures, situations. Miss Elizabeth Haven's afternoon teas would do very well just now, in an interim; she did not disdain them; but she chafed at dull proprieties and averaged pleasures. She consoled herself with the anticipation of gayer, freer things; with fun at large, and the chance and test of it, that were coming soon, in the great yearly picnic to Shepaug.

This had been talked of one afternoon at Miss Haven's. In a week or two it would come off. Everybody would be there; everybody always was; it was the last festival afield of the season.

"It is the great event of Wewachet; and there is nothing so lovely as Shepaug," some one said to Putnam King, taking his attendance for granted, and describing to him the delights he might expect. "You 'll be with us, of course, Miss Haven?"

"I am afraid not.   I am to be with friends in
Newport at about that time."

"Oh, don't!   Come back for the day, at least.
You must n't miss it, and we can't miss you.   We
want Mr. King, too."

"I 'm not much good at a picnic," said Mr.
King, laughing. "They always have seemed to
me like Dickens's circumlocution office, — a how-
not-to-do-it sort of institution.   You can't get the
things you want to eat, and you can't find the people you want to see, and the lovely ·place you go
to is n't there ; it 's all blotted out by the crowd."

"All the more reason you should go with us to
Shepaug.   We manage things differently ; and
Shepaug can't be blotted out."

"I dare say ; I have great confidence in you,"
returned Mr. King, smiling.   Connie Norris came
up with a little rush.   "Shepaug?" she cried.
"Oh, I would n't miss it for a farm !   No, not for
a copper mine, or a whole western railroad !   Dr.
Harriman, *you* have never seen Shepaug."

Dr. Harriman, taken *en passant*, like a pawn at
chess, stopped perforce.

"Oh, yes, Miss Connie.   I have driven there,"
he said.

"Indeed, you can't have half seen it that way,"
rejoined Miss Connie.   "The loveliest walks and
climbs and views !   Why, Mr. King was objecting to

the crowd. You would n't know a crowd was there, except right in the middle. We all go our own way, and the only trouble is which way to choose."

" Or *whom* to choose as fellow pilgrim," said the lady who was talking with Putnam King, as Connie and the doctor moved along a little toward Miss Haven and the teacups. " It is just the place for a good, honest, open-air flirtation."

" Is there such a thing ? " inquired Mr. King.

" As what? The thing, or such quality of the thing ? "

" What is flirtation ? "

" Really, it is very undefinable. Miss Haven, this innocent young man wants to know what flirtation is. Suppose we resolve ourselves into a debating society and find out. Don't you know, Miss Connie ? "

Connie Norris laughed. " We 're in a library. There's a Webster's dictionary here, somewhere, I suppose," she answered, not unreadily.

" Very well, let us put it to Webster, then. Only it will be like picking a field flower out of a herbarium."

" Oh, really ! " exclaimed Putnam King. " That *is* defining it beforehand with a coolness and fresh- ness. That is imputing innocence and simplicity at once."

" Yes. I don't mean the cut-and-dried article,

bear in mind. There *is* a fresh and innocent sort."

"May be. If you look far enough back for it, in the early and unconscious years. But I thought we were speaking of men and women, — of a good, honest, recognized thing."

"You hold to your point with a legal exactness. Well, we will concede it, — I did mean that; only I spoke of young people, not case-hardened old stagers."

"I see. There must be lines; it all depends upon where you draw them."

"Of course. And that is what our survey is for. Dr. Harriman, won't you look?"

Dr. Harriman had no choice. The big dictionary was at his elbow.

"What is it?" asked the impatient lady the moment he ceased furling the leaves.

"'Playing at courtship,' Mrs. Sudley," the doctor answered, clearly and unabashed. Brought to bay, Dr. Harriman could face the occasion. "But that is not an inside definition, I think. It is the statement of a looker-on. Dr. Webster probably never flirted."

A gentle, musical laugh was the rejoinder. "Shall we look to you for an inner interpretation, Dr. Harriman?" and the laugh broke out, irresistibly, around him.

With a perfectly composed face Dr. Harriman met the assault. Connie Norris, who had shrunk a little backward, was all pink and fluttering, like a breeze-shaken rose.

"I should say it might be 'tentative acquaintance,' Mrs. Sudley," Dr. Harriman replied.

"And the question is, how much of that is allowable?"

"Precisely, I suppose."

"Mr. King, it is your turn. You raised the point."

"From all that I have ever seen of the thing, I should say it was 'a self-defeating experiment.'"

"Oh, that won't do! That is more outside. You are worse than Webster."

"You could hardly expect me to try an inside view, holding such a theory, Mrs. Sudley?"

"Mr. King, I prophesy for you a brilliant career at the bar. But won't you explain?"

"I think Dr. Harriman's argument, in the nature of the case, should have precedence."

"I do not know that I have undertaken any case. The demand upon me seems rather of the character of a subpœna," said Dr. Harriman, with careless good-humor.

"Very well; bear witness, doctor," said Mrs. Sudley, gayly. "Yet, after all, it is a debate, you see, not a case in court. Now don't pun; we want serious work."

Perhaps Dr. Harriman was not sorry to define indirectly his own position.

" Seriously, then, Mrs. Sudley," he said to her, with an air that might carry gracefully either jest or earnest, " I do not see, unless we are to rush blind-fold into matrimony, or adopt French customs and leave arrangements to our ancestors, why we should not be entitled to what I call ' tentative acquaint-ance.' I don't see how we are to do without it."

" What do you call ' tentative acquaintance,' Dr. Harriman ? " questioned Putnam King.

" Why, a certain degree of intimacy ; a certain amount of " — he hesitated.

" Monopoly ? " suggested Mr. King.

" Well, yes, if you put it so," replied the doctor, laughing. " Some chance to try sympathies, and find out character, and prove how much or how little two persons may like and suit each other. But if there is to be watching and outcry, and the whole community either down upon them or forcing their affairs to a conclusion, then — I don't see what becomes of the preamble to the Declaration of Independence of these United States."

" Or of any united state at all," said Mrs. Sud-ley, laughing.

" You punned ; I did n't," quoth the doctor.

Mrs. Sudley turned to Mr. King. " Dr. Harri-man has explained ' tentative acquaintance,' " she

said. " Suppose you instruct us as to how it is a
' self-defeating experiment ' ? "

Putnam King was absolutely grave. His boyish
banter was laid aside. At this moment he seemed
the maturer of the two men. " I think," he said,
" by being a trying on of an intimacy that is not expected necessarily to last. There isn't any real test
in it. It assumes what was first to be found out ;
leaving, as the only thing to be found out, the probable mistake. I think acquaintance needs to be
a slower, more mixed, process; that people should
see each other in their other relations, where the
play of character comes out. Monopoly, through
a mere passing attraction, is n't acquaintance at
all. Two persons are just what they choose to seem
to each other, for the sake of pleasing. It is n't a
fair thing, especially to a woman."

" Where is the unfairness, if it is understood as
tentative ? " asked Dr. Harriman.

" In that very understanding," replied Putnam
King.

When the little company had broken up, the two
young men, at Dr. Harriman's suggestion, took
leave together, lighted their cigars outside, and
walked in the twilight down toward the Point.

" How much of that was earnest, King ? " asked
the doctor, as they went along.

" All of it," replied Putnam King, instantly.

" How much of it was meant for me ? "

" As much as belongs.   As much as you 'll take.
As much as you need."

" Thanks.   But perhaps my appropriation might
be in the way of somebody else getting a fair share.
There are girls who will flirt, my friend."

" Then I think the question of tentative acquaintance would be set aside.   But I only speak for myself.   The girl whom I marry will be the girl who
won't flirt."

" The definite article is well put.   There may
be one such girl to a half dozen square miles of
civilization.   I 'm of your mind, precisely ; but the
world is small ; we might run against each other."

How much was meant, or understood, neither
knew as regarded the other.   Each thought for
himself, however, that he had learned something.

Meanwhile, two young women who had listened
to the tea-table debate with more or less of self-
application, were recalling it with characteristically
different impressions.

Connie Norris drew from it a certain comfortable logical inference.   It gave her quite a little
elastic inward spring to think of the "tentative
acquaintance " between herself and Dr. Harriman.
With his definition of the thing, there must have
been in it something of meaning, of possible purpose.   What, then, had signified the recent with-

drawal? Was it caution, or retreat? Connie
wished she knew. She had been very frigid and
unfeeling elsewhere lately; she had gone as far
that way as she safely could. She had no mind to
fall between two stools. Her fancy had been
taken with Dr. Harriman, but he might not mean
anything, while George Craigan did. Moreover,
though she might appease young Craigan with
surreptitious little relentings, and bring him back
at her pleasure to full devotion, it would be harder
to satisfy George Craigan, *père*, if this stigma of
flirt got fastened upon her by too flagrant derelic-
tion. And the approval of George Craigan, *père*,
— the solid, old-fashioned, money-strong and will-
strong head of the family and firm, into the latter
of which the son had just been received, and which
stood upon old hereditary foundations begun away
back before gold and telegraphs and railroads, and
prosperous all the way down through all the
changes and magnifications of business, — was an
essential element in the calculation. Connie Norris was a featherhead; but she was not exactly a
fool.

Cyrilla Raye said to herself, recalling Putnam
King's words, which had fallen upon some newly
developed sensitiveness within her: "The play of
character — to be studied by seeing a girl in her
other relations. What sort of study would anybody

make of me, that way, I wonder, — a girl who never had any real, right relations? I have got them all to make, new, before I shall be real, — before I shall have fair play ; and who is going to believe it of me ? Life is not fair, in this world ! We are begun at the wrong end, so many of us ! But then, if there is a wrong end, I suppose it is in ourselves, to begin with, or we should n't be where we are. What is — or ever was — the beginning? Why am I Rill Raye ? "

CHAPTER X.

FOLKS AND " CREETURS."

PUTNAM KING had arrived at Crooke Corner at one of his irregular times, and had found that his aunt Elizabeth was absent.

The unfailing sign of the close-drawn gray shades did not escape him as he approached the house; but his step did not slacken, nor his face take on any blankness. It might have been with a not uncheerful sense of other possibilities that he kept on his way, and without making evidence of himself by any needless inquiry, went rather quietly upstairs to the library and settled himself to patient waiting. Why he chose a seat somewhat retreated from the diminished light and half shielded from the rest of the apartment by a large picture upon an easel, may not be a relevant consideration; the result was, however, that not long after, Miss Cyrilla Raye came lightly up-stairs and into the room where she had been bidden to make herself welcome at all times; and, quite unconscious of any other presence, pursued her evident errand by going directly across to the opposite bookshelves, where she put up a volume she had brought, and began to examine others of the same set that stood in line with it.

Putnam King knew that they were certain of the writings of the deep truth-searcher, Swedenborg. He was interested to observe how far her investigations would go in this direction, and whether, having had one dip into occult themes, she would resolve immediately upon a second. He waited until she had chosen her book, which she did after slightly turning the leaves of several that she took down and put back in succession. Then she slipped into a cushioned chair in the east window close by, rolling the Holland shade partly up as she did so. She had committed herself to her intention, opening her book and beginning at its first page, when Putnam King spoke ingenuously.

" I won't interrupt you, Miss Raye," he said ; " but it seems fair you should know I 'm here. Now please go on with your book. I won't speak again, if you don't choose. I 've got an article here in the ' Fortnightly.' "

Apparently this young man acted up to his theories when he had the chance.

Rill had made a movement to start up ; then she checked herself.

" I don't know that I shall go on," she said,

coolly. "I just wanted to make up my mind. When I have done that I shall go off, thank you."

"Could I help you?" he asked, politely, seeing instantly his only possibility. What he wanted, of course, was to study the play of this young lady's character in relation to books. The decisions of Miss Raye would but be precipitated, he was well aware, by resistance; the making up of her mind might be pleasantly, as well as wisely, prolonged. He ventured forward as he spoke, and glanced, as with a first notice, at the gap on the shelf, and at the corresponding volume in Cyrilla's hand.

"What has sent you to Swedenborg?" he asked, in kindly, curious tone.

"I don't know that I am sent," she answered. "I was reading Miss Phelps, first. I went 'Beyond the Gates,' with her; and then I tried 'Heaven and Hell.' One was an imagination; I thought I should like to see what an authority would say."

"Do you fancy those researches?"

"I 've had just about enough of this world to want to find out what any other world might be like."

"And your conclusions?"

"The only thing I 've come to — it is n't a conclusion, nothing is, I suppose — is an idea that Swedenborg *did n't* get beyond the gates."

"How do you mean?"

" I mean the whole of it is right here, without
going out of this world for it. As far as I can
find out from the book, there is n't any more
Heaven than might be now, if people behaved
themselves; and — well, on the whole — as they
don't, I think this is probably one of the more re-
spectable sort of hells. People are made as comfortable as they can be, and they are kept under
by laws and punishments. It answers to the description exactly."

King laughed. " You are a most original inter-
preter," he said.

" I wonder it never occurred to anybody before
— if it did n't," Rill answered, with composure.
" I think I 'll take this, and see if I can make
anything more out of the ' Wisdom of the Angels.' " She closed the book in her hand, and got
up to go. Evidently, she would not be beguiled
into forgetting that purpose.

Mr. King took another book from a higher shelf,
where were recent additions of fresher works.
" You will like this, I think," he said ; and offered
her Drummond's " Natural Law in the Spiritual
World."

" Thank you." She merely glanced at the title.
" I will remember it for next time," she said ; and
passed him with the sweetest smile of pertinacity,
without another word, but only a bowed good-by.

She was on the stairs. The front door closed behind her. Mr. King stood still a moment ; then he replaced the postponed Drummond, caught up his hat, went out through the little passage into which a further door opened, and crossing from that through the room devoted to his own use upon his visits, descended unobserved a narrow, twisted stairway, and made exit from the house into the orchard behind. He thought it would be better to arrive again, when he should have taken a little walk.

The chestnut wood invited him, with its broad leafage beginning to turn golden in some places, its soft tracks leading down into deeply shaded hollows where the chestnuts ended and old pines sent up their columns in multiplied sweet vistas, and squirrels flashed from turf to summits, and far off the hermit thrush whistled a late, lonely song. Between the North Road and the Corner this forest bit lay wild and beautiful.

As he went along his thoughts pursued the study of a character which had given them an occupation of late increasingly attractive ; this occupation itself, very likely, suggesting much towards the shaping of his notions to definiteness as concerning means and methods in that sort of observation.

"She is no flirt," he said to himself for something like the twentieth time since he had first heard Rill Raye's name, and begun to compare hearsay with illustration. " She disdains the common opportunities; or is it that finer coquetry of nature which will not make them, but waits that they shall be made? I wish I knew if that nicer coquetry would influence her toward me. — if some delicate instinct of it might lie in her somewhat rigorous reserves." In such wise, without set words, his reflections ran. " It is a shame these people should translate her by their own little miserable vocabulary ! "

That last thought did speak plain. He repeated the four first words with a force that from a different man's mouth would have had a garnish. But Putnam King did not use garnish. Instead he kicked a clod that lay in his path very vigorously out of his way.

" What kind of a world is she shut up into, in the midst of all that is beautiful like this, and that might be dear and bright to her, that she should say what she did of the world just now ? A fellow would like to take a case like that in hand for a good, strong holding up — and setting down."

There was a hint of the young lawyer in this, — a hint, at least, of the enthusiasm of justice which ought to make a lawyer. But when a man takes up in eager imagination the rights and interests of a charming young woman, the cliency and counsel he imagines are very near an identification of cause.

Walking in the chestnut wood, and on down into the pines, his thought, and others that belonged and asserted themselves with it, grew and grouped, and kept him beautiful new company. A presence had come to him ; and life in this green delight between two dusty roads looked lovely to him. The best things in us — the best that we have or dream of — do not need instant or continual presentment in their outer fact. We go away with a word or a glimpse, and it becomes to us, in a blessed interval when nothing can contradict, a whole possession and experience. If people only knew how often the glimpses are best, and would not foolishly thrust themselves upon each other ! It was this that Putnam King had sense of in the feeling that lay beneath his theories of tentative acquaintance. But this spiritual tact, which is the " finer coquetry," belongs to very few. So the world crowds and crushes and blunts out what it was meant to illustrate, less with outright showing than with exquisite reserves.

Whatever it was that had worked in Cyrilla Raye to put her at this unconscious advantage, it had worked in the higher ranges of her nature ; not at all in that region of her which had used to concern itself with her gay little passing relations, and with the contingent possibilities to which they might some time lead. There was none of the speculation, or the whim, in it, that would have made it a form of coquetry ; rather it was a humility — a self-depreciation — born in her with the impression that had come to her of fairer things. She was held back from such nonsense as she might have fallen into a while ago, by new realities that had entered her life. Her eager, repressed affections had poured themselves out on Miss Haven, whose kindness had won her to such admiration and gratitude as could satisfy themselves with nothing less than growing worthy, — becoming what could dare to be transparent before such reading and judgment as her friend's were sure to be.

This feeling in her was an absolute prophylactic against any temptation to silliness where Putnam King might be concerned ; even if, besides, she had not experienced such a sense of sphere — not mere worldly, but made up of just those realities which she had begun to know and long for — that divided her, as yet, from these persons so different from any she had come in close contact with before.

She was too busy with herself in these days to play the part of mimic self, which is the experiment of vanity. She had never lost, for a moment, the strange effect and inspiration of that " pond

lily room." Its lesson had gone straight to the
best and truest in her. A white stateliness, a
sweet, delicate pride, a fearless uplifting from all
that was low and common into beautiful, searching
light, — these seemed to her now the things to
be striven — to be prayed for. She was scornful
of her old self when she thought about it.

And yet, there was quite the chance that through
this very awakening she might make a vital mistake. She would long to live her idea, the more
that it was so fast outgrowing her present sur-
rounding, — so essentially changing herself. A
girl often marries as she might even die — in the
hope of a new life that she may live more excel-
lently. It is the next chance and change for her.
It is a change of worlds.

A larger judgment had before this convinced
Cyrilla Raye that there was nothing of meaning,
nothing that could last with either, perhaps, in the
relations between Dr. Harriman and Connie Norris. It was not the deep and lifelong reality that
it would be such treachery to interfere with or di-
vert. Interference would not even be worth while.
A surer thing would finish it with Connie any
day; it had flagged already to her weariness; she
would not wait through much uncertainty; she
would not take the trouble to be disappointed. It
was but a question of brief time.

Cyrilla had been quick enough to perceive also that if she chose to allow it, Dr. Harriman would very readily displace — she would not deign to think of it as a transference — his trifling attentions to Cornelia Norris by a more quiet and dignified approach toward herself. Her expostulation with him, which had been prompted rather by a care for Connie's place in general estimation than by fear for her peace of mind, had resulted in simply strengthening her in this sense of the matter.

She felt that Dr. Harriman liked to be with her; that he respected her, — she had accomplished that; that he sought, at least, to become her friend. In the refined, intelligent intercourse of Miss Haven's chosen little circle, she knew that he appreciated her; she discerned, also, the best of him. If she compared him involuntarily with Putnam King, that sense of sphere interposed directly, and for her own safety she shrunk back from a possible preference or attraction that could only disappoint. The one was within her reach, the other she might not so much as question about, and she did not. She did not even ask herself if there were danger. She shut her eyes mentally, in pride, and walked on; only guarding herself carefully from least seeming to account herself as of account with him. And so, unconsciously, she was already commanding him, as we and he are finding out. Kill Raye

would be long in imagining such a thing possible.
Long after she might have gained that " transparent worthiness " she had learned to covet, she
would still have held herself in the old scorn. Her
aunt Amelia had done her this terrible injustice
of " mortifying her ; " of " touching her pride " in
that deadly way which destroys a pure self-confi-
dence.

Putnam King came back from his wood walk
with certain things in him grown clearer and more
purposeful. He was the richer for his purposes.
His faith in life was warm and strong, grasping
the substance of things hoped for.

In such mood he lingered before entering the
house. He turned his steps around its westward
side, and paused when he came to an old-fashioned
settee-rocker that stood in a blank space against
the clapboards. It could not rock : it was bedded
in green turf and pushed close up to the building.
Within was Miss Sarah's sitting-room. If he passed
the door that opened just beyond upon the grass-
plot, he would be seen and hailed. He stopped
here and sat down. Presently he would go back
and enter the other way. He thought he would
have a talk with aunt Elizabeth to-night.

But aunt Elizabeth was not in yet, and he felt
deliciously lazy. Warm shade and softened glow
were all about him. Miss Crooke had set her

" yard door," as she called it, open, and he could hear the short creak of her rockers as she sat near it and vibrated herself gently to and fro. The world was in sweet humor, and he was in sweet humor with the world; except with that piece or aspect of it which had sent Rill Raye among Swedenborg's hells to locate her own planet.

If that strange insight of hers touched any truth, there was at least this comfort in it. The " great gulf fixed," was not impassable to all angel feet. World interpenetrated world — or might do so.

He began to see the beauty of his aunt Elizabeth's coming here. Surely she had already brought some lights and airs of paradise. The murk had cleared away from the round of her own atmosphere; she was making a horizon of her own. Crooke Corner was becoming a little Ararat, whence the evil floods were subsiding, and a sweet greenness was lifting up. Sarah Crooke was learning to look with her beautiful eye. He thought that, perhaps, he would go in and see Miss Sarah, presently, for a moment, before he went upstairs.

But while he sat there, a change came upon Ararat. A cloud dropped over it. A surf of the old, turbid deep swept in.

Miss Sarah's rockers hitched about with a heavy shove. The quiet was broken by sharp, high tones of voices that had only learned to speak from the tops of lungs or of souls ; upon Putnam King's ear there jarred the thin surface cackle that he had perceived to belong generically to the sort of human creatures who seem in the great round of evolution to have latest and most imperfectly achieved humanity. They enter its ranks from various lower stages of approach, more or less harmful or innocent of nature ; these two whom he heard now were of cruel, predatory life, by heredity and selection.

Mrs. Porbeagle and Mrs. Sharke were second-cousins, in the first place. Then they were double sisters-in-law, each having married the other's brother. Character tendencies were strongly developed by birth and environment. For a Sharke to become a Porbeagle, and a Porbeagle a Sharke, was to intensify strain in a way only adequately illustrated by a doubling of force, in a high potential electric current.

What they did not take hold of, throw light upon, decompose, scorch, shock and slay in Wewachet, was simply beyond their circuit, or any malignant crossing of their wires.

I am not going to accuse Mr. King by excusing him. He heard plainly enough the talk that followed, and he did not rise up and go away. If the women had discussed their own affairs, he would have done so at once and gladly ; or if they

had not begun forthwith to deal out upon the air
with the freedom which premised that the air was
welcome to it, and might do what it would with it,
the report-current of Wewachet, he might have
felt more scruple; as it was, he lingered.

I am not going to set you listening to it all with
him, my reader. I have changed my mind about
that, though I could make you hear every word
that was said. It is enough to have one to excuse,
and the Sharke and Porbeagle atmosphere is not
pleasant to tarry in. I would have nothing to say
about it at all, but that we need to know and be
reminded to what stratum, and to what develop-
ment of pestiferous life, the germs fall finally that
are blown often through cleaner places by thought-
less breaths that know not what they circulate.
Everything that fell into the Porbeagle apprehension straightway took coarsest, or most venomous
form, and raised its head, presently, to poison,
hiss and sting.

So what Mr. King heard them say and re-
hearse here to-day, was result and deduction from
any slightest little remote floats of talk, that so
much as touched a failing or hinted a possibility
of error or mistake. These had materialized to
statement, taken positive shape in malice. From
poor little Mrs. Rospey's domestic tempers that
had become standard chronicle, and had now

passed into current report of her present slavery
to a mightier, if quieter, dominance in Lucretia
Dawse, who, "whatever had ailed the woman in
her old tantrums, had got the upper hand of
her now;" with the dark charity of a hint that
they "*did n't* believe the ailing was anything
she used to keep in the cupboard," — to Mrs.
Sholto and her stepson, the latter lately returned
from Europe, and the wonderful harmony between
the two, — "quite devoted; almost seems as if it
might have turned out full as suitable if she'd
waited awhile before taking the colonel," — and
then on, to Connie Norris and her "chasing" of
Dr. Harriman, — the miserable, irresponsible quot-
ing of "they says" and implications of "they
might says," continued. It was broken once, to
Putnam King's exulting delight, by an interjection
from Miss Sarah.

"*They say!*" she repeated with exceeding
scorn. "Then why don't *you* stop saying, Harriet
Porbeagle? What do you go trundling it round
for?"

An amazed silence followed; then it rippled
into speech again, begun more mildly, but soon
lapsing, by unconquerable tendency, into similar,
slightly diverted channels. And it was now that
it came close to Putnam King, — perhaps while it
was meant, covertly, as a little revenge upon Miss
Sarah Crooke.

" Rill Raye has n't turned still and stiff for nothing ; she knows what she 's about. She 's cunninger than Con Norris. It 's a ring-around-a-rosy, this chasing or being chased ; only depends on the distance you pretend to keep, for the look of the thing. Rill Raye knows how to lag back, and chase too. It 's a circus, anyway."

Here Miss Crooke made her little mistake. It was an overdoing of her championship, whence came afterward a shadow of mischief. " I don't know what you mean about Rill Raye," she said, " but I can tell you this : if she wanted — anybody — she 'd only need to take 'em. I know one or two that I guess stands pretty near ready."

Some impatient, contemptuous sound escaped Putnam King's lips ; he started up, and his heel struck the ground with a stamp, grazing a soft, comfortable fuzzy coil that lay hidden beneath the rocker. The great gray cat sprang out with forcible syllabic remonstrance, and rushed past the open door, his back arched and his tail big.

" What 's that ? " Mrs. Porbeagle exclaimed, within.

" It 's George Washington," Miss Crooke answered. " There 's something round he don't like ; I don't know whether it 's folks or creeturs. He 's a very sincere cat ; he always speaks himself right out."

With George Washington to cover his retreat, Mr. King withdrew in good order; but it was a pity he could not have heard Miss Sarah's explanation.

The talk that he thought he would have with his aunt that night resolved itself into two or three brief sentences at bedtime. They had played chess together, he had read aloud to her an article from Scribner's; they had spoken of half a dozen different things, but not till he stood up to say good-night did the words come that showed some flash of what had been burning unspoken in him all the while.

"Aunt Elizabeth, I think this world is getting to be — to have places in it — that it isn't fit a real, sweet, delicate woman should be born into. They talk of climate changing; it's more than that. I believe it is what Miss Raye called it this afternoon."

"What did she call it?" Miss Haven asked, passing by all surprise, or inquiry of the afternoon.

"She said it was just after the description of one of Swedenborg's hells."

Aunt Elizabeth was silent. She was not curious for disquisition; what she was curious for she thought it quite as prudent not to ask about.

"Aunt Elizabeth, Rill Raye needs to be taken care of. She needs to belong to somebody who can change her world for her."

"I suppose she does so belong," said Miss Haven to that, gravely. "But we human beings need to be very careful what we assume or undertake as regards each other's worlds."

"Suppose a human being finds his own world getting involved?"

"Then I think the human being should be all the more careful, and wait until he is pretty sure of everything."

"Ah, you forget the 'human,' though we have been saying it all the time," returned Putnam, laughing. But he did not say any more that night of all he had thought he had to say.

Perhaps he had said enough ; and perhaps Miss Elizabeth had given him the wisest and kindliest answer possible. At any rate, he feared to provoke by persistence or haste a less tolerant one.

In those same evening hours, the Porbeagles and the Sharkes had got together at the Hammerheads (*q. v.*, Encyc. Brit.) for a game of whist and a lobster salad. In the symposium over these, it was asserted, as an authentic piece of information, that Rill Raye had her choice of two offers, — from Dr. Harriman and from young lawyer King.

"Then Dr. Harriman is a shameful jilt!" cried young Mrs. Sphyrna Hammerhead, tempestuously. "And I wish somebody would just tell him so!"

"I shouldn't crave the job," said her husband,

dropping his heavy under jaw with a cold, hard laugh.

But the word was spoken and went on its way. Of course it drifted down to the Point, eddied back to Crooke Corner, and even swept around the North Road, where Miss Bonable heard it. And the view she took of it was not comfortable for Rill Raye.

CHAPTER XI.

THE time had arrived for the picnic to Shepaug. All Wewachet was full of it. The odor of preparation was in everybody's oven or boiler. The odor of anticipation was in thoughts and talk. The pulse of pleasure, hope, anxiety, was in heart and vein with several. It was to be a point of history with some. Therefore we must go to Shepaug, reader, whether you like picnics or not.

Dr. Harriman was going. It would be very unpopular to stay away. Besides which, it would not mend his present matters, and he felt they were in some need of mending. Something might even be advanced. judiciously, toward a future, fine, " far-off event" which he had begun to perceive he might desire ; which he meant, gradually, to place himself in a fair position to desire, and to realize, when the time should come ; though he still said to himself, with a steadfastness not altogether unworthy, that the time might not be yet. He thought he could gently smooth the way for it ; set his face, even, in that direction, so that he might be first upon the road. He did not suppose that any other, younger man, with no actual start in the world, would be in greater obvious hurry than himself.

He knew what people were saying ; he knew the complications into which he had fallen ; these meddling interferences would make it yet more difficult for him to place things exactly as he wished they should stand. For that very reason, he must take some initial measures at once. He wished, at any rate, to be a gentleman, to put himself into the attitude of one. There should be no more flirting with Connie Norris ; there could be nothing decisive elsewhere ; but he would like to explain himself a little to Rill Raye. That was as far as he had got in his determinations. We shall see how he succeeded in carrying them out.

Connie Norris was going, as we know. Nothing short of broken bones, or a serious illness, would detain her. She regarded it as a crisis. It would be such opportunity as must bring out whatever valued opportunity, or show plainly that the value was not there. She was tired of railway trains, and the necessity for purpose too resolved and conspicuous in its demonstration to be expected before fixed rows of eyes. The free solution of a merry company in the wide spaces of Shepaug would be better, and would offer surer test. If nothing crystallized there, the fault would be in elementary attraction.

Connie Norris made up her prettiest toilet, took care of herself to be in her prettiest looks, and put her fortune " to the touch, to win or lose it all." She did not " fear her fate too much," for, in the worst result, there would be George Craigan, the fine old place, and " the business" of which he was never tired of talking, now that he was in it and, as he thought, " *magna pars*." It was a rather nice lodgment of jackstraws to handle, undeniably. Connie was fluttered a bit when she thought of it ; but it was a difficulty to stimulate the delighted dexterity of a thorough little flirt, which Connie Norris was. If she *could* pick out the prize piece from the pile ! And if only they would not joggle !

She had heard the talk about Cyrilla Raye and her two offers, but it did not trouble her very much. The story went too far. She knew very well there had not been two offers. She did not believe there would be ; Rill Raye did not know how to manage matters, for all her tacks and turns. She was more in love with old Miss Haven than anybody else, and with making herself up to old Miss Haven's standard. Connie had penetration enough to see this, from outside evidence, far as she was from sympathetic understanding.

It only made her own little game of jackstraws more exciting; there would be the delight of puzzling, and perhaps surprising, all Wewachet. She was spurred, but in no whit discouraged.

Cyrilla Raye was neither satisfied nor expectant. It was always herself that she quarreled with, and she looked for no beautiful thing that should befall her or surprise anybody. Why should any such thing come which could only come by force of that in her which she knew she had not? She would not care for liking that was drawn to what she was; she did not like or approve of herself, as she compared herself with the ideal growing in her, and gathered from such different being. Perhaps before she could stand out in the light — the very " light of the living " — in which the regard she might imagine as worth while could come to her and claim her, she would have to live out all her disciplinary years in such companionship as might happen. She might have to content herself with the less, knowing that all it could be to her would be but a shadow of the greater. Was this what her piece of the world was meted to her for, just now and here? Was this why she was Rill Raye?

She was displeased with herself for the truest things she had done, because of her way of doing them. Why had she been so rough and blunt with

Dr. Harriman? Why should she have taken upon herself, in such outright fashion, to rebuke or set him right, when there was so much to set right in her own self? It was her own self she had thought of when she had said the hardest thing was self-blame; but it had not seemed or sounded so, she knew. Why could she do nothing except with an outbreak and extravagance?

What had she snubbed Putnam King for, because she did not choose to stay there talking with him alone, as Connie Norris might have done? Connie Norris would at least have been sunny and merry and pleasant. Why must Kill Raye, in trying to reject a silliness of character, reject with it all that was sweet and gracious; casting off one sort of person that she had resolved she would not be, without taking on the likeness or reality of a higher sort? Why could she not say and do things as — Margaret Rextell, or any girl that might be invited into that pond lily room — would do them?

"Why do I always take the bull by the horns, — with aunt Amelia, and all?" she demanded of herself. "Why could n't I have been civil for a minute or two with Mr. King, and then walked off, all the same? It was just as if I thought he needed to be — I wonder what he thought about it! And — I don't care!" She grew incoherent and angry, and foolishly mendacious with herself.

She told herself also that she did not care for these last rumors that had got afloat, and which had caused aunt Amelia to feel in duty bound to " mortify " her afresh.

" A girl does n't get talked of that way, unless she talks — or acts — herself," was what Miss Bonable had said ; and although it did not hurt Rill as accusation from her aunt, it did thrust deep with a misgiving of what Mr. King might think if the word had reached him. But she " did not care." No, — she would not care for anything. What was the use? A girl's life was hard, that was all. And this world was — well, it was not heaven, certainly.

It was in this mood that she went to Shepaug.

Miss Haven was away at Newport ; and Putnam King was off also. If there had been anybody whom he really cared to talk to — in libraries, by chance — Rill Raye thought he would have cared to come, and find the person here, in these places where to walk and talk would be so beautiful. But he had gone off to Newport, or somewhere else ; he disliked picnics ; and he did not care at all. He was very likely offended with her, to begin with ; he was not such a one as would need, or take, twice snubbing. She had done her duty bravely, but she had done it with a rudeness. Clearly, she was not in the same range with what she most appreciated and desired. She was just nowhere. And so she had shown herself to be, and Mr. King had seen it. On the top of all, had come this impertinent buzz about him. No wonder he had gone to Newport, or the Adirondacks, or wherever it was.

Well — it made no difference. Things would not have been otherwise, anyway. All she could do was to keep on with what she had, and be — what she was able. Perhaps by the time she was forty or fifty years old, she might have made her own individual place, and become some sort of individual creature that she would not be ashamed of. It was not in Rill Raye to sit down and despair. She would not have done it if she had been assured that her theories upon the Swedenborgian system were true. There were birds and sunshine, clear air and running water in the world, evil place though it had got to be through human importation. And there were human spots of excellent sweetness in it yet, she knew. She might come to some of them by and by, that would own her and take her in. She had Miss Haven now. She was sure of Miss Haven through all report; and she would not misuse her favor. But she would go to see her in the mornings, she thought, for a time.

There were green woods and birds and sunshine and bright waters at Shepaug. Very well; then Shepaug had something for her, even if all We-wachet were there too. She would simply go to Shepaug, for Shepaug itself, and let the pickers and the nickers take care of themselves.

Putnam King stayed away from Wewachet. He did not care, for his own part, for the word that was running round there. But he would not sub-ject Rill Raye to any more observation or annoy-ance. He would not let her think he had had any chance to hear. He would turn the tide of gossip if he could. By and by he could come again. In his own way, and at the right time, he could speak his own word.

He accompanied his aunt to Newport, and then went to join some friends for a week or two in the Adirondacks. It would be his last lengthened holiday for a good while. In November he was to enter a law office, where the chief was among the foremost in his profession, and where a young man might look for advancement in his work as fast as he could take it. There was business over-flowing into other hands, continually; Mr. Arbi-con would not have more than two regularly in-stalled under him at a time; but those two, he said, must be of the sort to come up alongside.

The bit of Shepaug which makes the pleasure

ground to which our friends repaired, is as pretty
a spot and as unlike anything but itself as can be
found among New England hills and streams.
Shepaug river makes a wonderful loop around a
pile of ledge and its marginal wooded slope and
level : tracing through the meadows a sign like
that of the Greek Omega, or the "eye" which
is made for a hook to catch.   It leaves almost
islanded — enough so for it to be called Shepaug
Island — the beautiful great green heap which
rears up from its watersides.   The river loop is
flung toward Wewachet ; it doubles and redoubles
itself opposite, at north and south of a narrow isth-
mus, which is little more than a broad roadway,
shrubbery-fringed, at once entrance and exit of the
drive which follows round the water line.

There are two ways of reaching Shepaug Island
from Wewachet : by carriage, around over one of
the two bridges at the North and South Mills, or
directly across by boat to a pretty landing on the
fair, outcurving hither bank.   The river is wide
and deep here, spreading up over the Wewachet
meadows ; the current widens and slackens, and is
safe to stem.   Many of the picnickers chose the
boating access ; but three great " barges " — those
curiously misnamed vehicles which sail overland
by horse power — conveyed a goodly number of
merry folk ; and all sorts of private conveyances,

from landaus and victorias to modest buggies and small wagonettes, complemented the further requirements, and made gay the Old West Road and the Otterbury Turnpike.

For ourselves, we need take neither way; we simply wish to be there; and with a thought-spring, we may alight among the rapidly assembling groups that are finding their relations and taking form and place here and there about the landing - head, or deeper in the pleasant wood glades; or up, with adventurous feet, along the sides and crest of the beetling ridge, upon its mossy rocks and among sweet-smelling cedars.

A young party had quickly established itself upon a well known jut, commanding and overlooking the lovely river bends, and uplifted into the soft, sunny air so high that it seemed doubly islanded, — by the fair waterflow far down, and by the buoyant ocean of the atmosphere. Here Dr. Harriman presently found Rill Raye, Connie Norris, Sue Wilder, with half a dozen other girls, and an escort of young men, among whom, closely attendant upon Connie Norris, was Mr. George Craigan, quite faultlessly attired in summer suit of gray, with a sprig of dull-green savin and its bloomy clusters of gray berries in his buttonhole.

Connie Norris had given it to him, as "just matching;" and then had set him off, with purposed mischief, upon his "hobby-stilts."

"I don't see how you could get away so early," she had said. "What will become of things in Berkshire street without you?"

"Oh, we have got nearly settled there; and it's a grand move, I can tell you, Miss Connie. We ought to have had that branch long ago. And there are other things we're thinking of — not quite matured as yet; but they'll lead to a good deal by and by. We're going to manage our foreign purchasing differently; I may be abroad next year," he added, lowering his voice to Connie's private ear, as a proper business reticence required.

"Ah, indeed?" the girl returned carelessly. "In that case, whom do you leave in your place here? I hope you find your father of considerable use to you in your business, Mr. George?" She raised her tone with the question; it was too good a hit not to have an audience.

Dr. Harriman came up in time to hear it. He turned a little, and lingered, postponing his greeting, while the half-restrained laugh followed which recognized the shrewdness of the sarcasm.

George Craigan was less obtuse in his conceit than he might have seemed. There was something of an honest dignity, as well as of provoked perception, in his reply.

"My father *is* the business," he answered her. "I am trying to be of use as fast as I can." And

with that, he also turned away a little. Connie
Norris was, for the moment, left at disadvantage.
But she recovered herself, with her invariable
light agility.

" Now that was very well put, George," she said,
making an easy little step and turn that brought
her facing him again. " I like it of you. You
must not mind my fun."

The calling him by his name, which she did now
and then with a reversion as of old habit to the
familiarity of their childhood, appeased him ; and
Connie could certainly put a witchery of coaxing
into her voice. But it was not altogether enough.
" I wish you were ever a little in earnest," he said ;
and then he really did turn off, speaking to Edith
Pinceley, and Connie could not persist.

" That was rather too bad," said Dr. Harriman
to Rill Raye. " The young man deserves better
of her."

" Perhaps he deserves better " — and then Rill
stopped.

" Than to have anything of her ? " and Dr. Harriman laughed gently.

" I do not think — we — have any right to say,"
returned Cyrilla, gravely, leaving Dr. Harriman
to Connie herself, who approached him gayly,
claiming him for some game they were about to
play.

" What game is it you propose, Miss Connie ? " asked the doctor.

" Candor," replied Connie, gleefully. " We 're to make everybody tell the truth about something, once. Come ! "

Cyrilla found herself a place a little way off, not quite separating herself from the others, but securing a slight isolation under the small shadow of a green cedar, into an angle of whose dividing stem she leaned comfortably. The air and light were very sweet about her. There was wide room, above, around, away from the little noisy human group which could take up but such trifling space and time here, where all had been so broad and still and leisurely before it came, and would be again after it had gone. There was rest and recompense in the perception ; she thought after all it was the secret thing that made the charm even to heedless people, bringing their pleasure out from their house walls into this great, rich, open world.

" See here ! " called Connie Norris's voice with gay intrusion ; " you shall have a fair alternative. You may guess a conundrum, or give a definition, instead. Question and word for the whole party at once. Ten minutes allowed for reflection. Here are paper and pencils. Each one is to hand in a written answer — or be put upon the stand !

Listen! — Oh, first, if any duplicate answers are given, — unless they are the right ones, — each person will have to pay the forfeit."

" Then wrong guesses will be permitted to count ? "

" Yes ; if they are real guesses ; if they have any point."

" Who shall decide the point ? " asked Dr. Harriman.

" Where there is any doubt, we will put it to the vote."

" And we may define — or divine — whichever we please ? "

" Yes ; but *definitions* are to be in verse."

" O — h ! "

" Now ! What was the first thing, that we know of, in the history of the world ? — that 's the conundrum ; — and, — What is a dude ? — that 's the creature to be defined."

" The first thing ? the first that was made, or that happened, or was done ? "

" Either, all three ; that 's your business."

" I wonder what her own is — in this invention," said Dr. Harriman to Rill Raye, beside whom he came and placed himself. " She will forget the conditions, in laying them down for us, and will fall under forfeit."

Rill thought it might be that was the purpose

Dr. Harriman queried about ; but she did not say so. She wrote three small words upon her bit of paper, folded it up, and let her thoughts wander again, quite away from the game and the company and Dr. Harriman, into questions of things harder and wider to conjecture and define than those Connie had propounded.

On his part, Dr. Harriman wrote three words also ; and then, glancing at Rill, and perceiving her abstraction, busied himself with another bit of paper and his pencil, somewhat to his own private amusement, it would appear, from the very slight play of eye and lip, which nobody, however, noticed.

" Time up ! " called George Craigan, whom Connie had graciously installed as her aid-de-camp.

The scraps of paper were collected, and George and Connie read them.

Rill recalled herself, and listened. All sorts of small epigrams were perpetrated, some of them feeble enough, of course.

"A garden party." "A delusion." "A legal argument." "An informal lunch." " A philosophical experiment." " An apple slump." "A mistake." " A confidence game." " A caucus." " A sewing circle." " A family move." " A woman's rights convention." "The Dude himself."

" Half of those won't do," remarked the doctor,

in another aside to Rill. " They presuppose something else."

" They won't find that out," said Rill. " And if they did, there 's always something back of everything. Where would be the end ? "

" Or the beginning? " said the doctor.

" Is there any difference? Which was presupposed ? "

" Ah, you go very deep, Miss Raye ! "

" I don't imagine this conundrum does. It is probably something very literal. There is the catch."

Rill was right. No answer was challenged ; people were satisfied to be amused even slightly.

" There are two answers identical," announced Miss Norris ; " Dr. Harriman's and Rill Raye's : ' The First Day.' They must pay the forfeit. And yet, they are nearest right of any. Why could n't you all see ? It was simply *a revolution.* What else *could* have happened first ? "

" Where is your answer, Miss Connie ? " demanded the doctor.

" Oh, I knew, you see."

" Then you must do as Eve did, — pay the penalty of your knowledge. But perhaps you have defined ? "

" No, I forgot. But I will."

" Too late. Time 's up."

There was an acclaiming laugh, and Connie accepted the position. " Very well? " she said, interrogatively, and awaited Dr. Harriman's question.

But Dr. Harriman turned to George Craigan. " Mr. Craigan has the best right," he said. " He leads the game — after yourself, Miss Connie. Mr. Craigan, what have you to ask Miss Norris? "

A smile ran round, and George Craigan blushed. Connie Norris looked a trifle provoked, and Dr. Harriman profoundly innocent.

" Miss Connie, what would you — really — like best of all things? " put the catechist, with a mild diffidence.

" To be *wild*ly adored! " answered Connie instantly.

The comical breadth with which she emphasized her frank audacity brought down upon her a peal of merriment, touched with applause.

" Rill Raye, what would *you* like best — really — of all things? " Connie passed the question quickly on.

" I think, to be really understood," said Cyrilla, gravely.

" Only another form of the same statement, possibly," commented Dr. Harriman, *sotto voce*, as quite involuntarily.

Cyrilla heard.

" Dr. Harriman, what would *you* like best?" continued Connie, eagerly.

"To understand — and to adore," the doctor answered, with most shrewd division, or combination, as it might be taken.

The Reverend Mr. Pinceley, who had rather blinked at the gay allusions to Mosaic records, took it *au grand sérieux.*

" A fine reply, Dr. Harriman," he said. " You have redeemed the play."

" I do not think I meant to — in your sense, Mr. Pinceley," said Dr. Harriman. " I merely put objectively the young ladies' subjective declarations."

" No answer at all, of your own, then!" cried Connie Norris triumphantly. " Your forfeit is not paid! What " —

But the doctor was too quick for her.

" I do not think I am really at all liable," he said. " I had a definition ready."

And Connie, recognizing that his first submission had been quite gratuitous, and to please himself, was obliged to receive his second folded paper which he offered her. The flicker of disappointment on her face, however, gave way to an irresistible smile, as she glanced over it and gayly read aloud, — " ' What is a Dude?'

" ' If I give you an answer pat and good
   Shall I win the conundrum cup?
 He 's a fellow who 's done all there is to be do-ed,
   And is all do-ed up ! ' "

In the shout which greeted this elucidation, the
doctor got up and walked off, with a leisurely in-
difference.

Cyrilla slipped away, also, to a yet further distance, beyond her clump of cedars, escaping the
merry clamor that followed, with confused proposi-
tions for fresh diversions, and the new game that
was presently insisted on and decided.

She went and seated herself at the edge of the
green bluff, with her feet upon a shelf of rock
below the brink. There was something here, better
than the nonsense game.

She looked off upon the calmly speeding river,
its grand, blue curve thrown out around the bold
promontory with beautiful embrace, — the meadow
and pasture lands, — the houses of the various village neighborhoods, dotting with their many tints
the open spaces, or showing with gleam of white
and red and olive and russet, or sunshiny yellows,
the warm blossoming of homes among the verdure;
the tender sky overarching all, and seeming, as one
looked down and up from this mid-perch, to lift
more magnificently and give larger room between
earth and heaven; the air, all luminous with soft

hazes, reflections of sweet tints from hill to hill along the horizon, and the already coming glory which was gathering in the westward-rolling tide of sunlight.

Cyrilla thought of rooms in the Father's house, made for different, happy needs and natures, — meant, each one, to meet and fulfill some answering beauty and truth of life that should be fit to dwell there; some soul of rose or lily, strength of oak, or healing health of pine, or generousness of maple, or even sweetness of lowly, faithful grasses; all typical, all full of a commandment and rebuke, as the pond lily room and the wild rose chamber in that gentle woman's house had been to her.

Yet up into God's air comes the smoke of strife and sin; in many a forest runs the savage beast; through tender grasses slips the serpent! What did it all mean? What hateful power worked in the world against the diviner life, perverting it to evil and mischance and pain and death? What contrariety worked in her own life that it was not a pure peace, an innocent joy, a rich satisfying in the midst of all these shows and signs of heaven?

She did not know how long the time was; she was shielded from the players, who had missed and called her for a moment, and then with shouts and laughter went on with their game. She was roused up when it was over by a final peal of merriment and a movement of the party, restless for some yet new plan.

They strolled off, away from the cliff, and down by a path upon the other side to the pine woods where the " sweet spring " and the late violets were.

Rill did not seem to care for either in so much company. She went back to the little beach and the boat landing, and busied herself with her aunt Amelia and the older people. Mr. Pinceley came and talked to her; she submitted with a more docile gravity than usual, so that the good man, believing in sudden heavenly changes, and watching solicitously for them among his flock, began to have gentle, kindly hope of Rill.

She missed Miss Haven. The picnic was dull; she would like best, if she could, to get away. I am afraid she did not even hear all that Mr. Pinceley was saying. It may be, however, that some teaching, as true and deep, was moving upon her own thoughts silently, and even informed stray words of the minister's, heard passively, with more than he put into them. We listen to sermons so.

Later in the afternoon, when she had helped Miss Bonable and Mrs. Rospey at the tables, she escaped again; she turned off from the pretty open glade where the repast was set, and followed the farmers' cart-track down among the woods. She had found her opportunity for a little solitude.

The social drift had set toward the river shore; all along the pebbly margin, below the fringes of wild shrubbery, went feet and voices. Some were skipping stones; some were taking to the boats to row up and down awhile; some sat idly in the low sunshine, talking, joking, anything.

Cyrilla wondered what it all amounted to. She had not used to wonder in such wise. She wondered at herself, most of all, what had come over her. It was as if all of a sudden she had the questions of her life to settle: why she was Cyrilla Raye; what, being Cyrilla Raye, she was to do with this personality she had charge of, and which it seemed so queer at once to manage and to be. There was something behind everything, as she had said before. What she really wanted was to understand herself.

The cart-track sloped down from a ridge spur over its crisp, moss-cushioned side, where the straight, thick savins lifted up their spicy bosks and made little nooks between their groups, to what seemed a plunge into deep, interminable woods; so tall and splendid grew the columnar pines, stretching their tasseled canopies overhead with interlacing arms, so that the blue patches of

sky gleamed through like shining inlay of turquoise
or *lapis lazuli;* and the sunlight, coming now in
oblique shafts from the west. struck in between
branch and bole and leafage with wonderful illumination, as through the windowed arches of a great
cathedral side.

Close under foot, just where Rill entered the for-
est-pile, grew in the damp hollow a broad bed of
low, matted, shining vines, the straight little stems
upholding each its cluster of glittering leaves of
darkest green, with finely serrated edges : the wild
strawberry plant that made a polished, tesselated
floor to this porchway of the woods. Rill gathered
a bunch and fastened it in the front of her gown ;
it lay against the soft, dull blue as the richness of
oak leaves shows against the tenderness of the sky.
She had put on a bit of the uniform of nature ;
somehow, it made her feel more harmonized with it
all. I think this innocent, natural sacrament is
partly what leaves and flowers are made for.
" These thy gifts and creatures," are all tokens
and signs ; the Holy Communion is in every created
thing. *Therefore*, woe to them who receive the
same unworthily ; who only adorn and surround
them*selves*, and so play with the husks that they
never find the bread !

Rill did not go far into the wood. She knew it
would not reach very much farther for her, in this

sweet illusion of depth. She knew it would come
out presently in sight of the two farmhouses that
were upon the island. She sat down upon a hum-
mock at the foot of a great oak which grew graciously among the pines, and watched the tiny mo-
tions of the growing things low down about her,
over which blew the soft breath of the hardly sensible air. They felt it, — the merest tremble of it,
and bent and quivered their little blades and bells;
or, perhaps, they thrilled to the touch and stir of
things yet tinier than themselves; of insect life
that ranged in the miniature forest of their stems.
Anyway, as Galileo said of the planet, they moved.
They were alive; and something else was all alive
about them. A little trickle from a hidden spring
ran its flashing thread in and out between. It
was not a brook, nor a rivulet, nor even a run; it
was only a creep of a few drops at a time, on their
slender way to find some larger water — which they
would find, Rill thought to herself. " I am glad
it is a live world, at least! " she said, aloud. All
at once that question came back to her, with a
sweet, curious suggestion in the syllables of her
own name.

" Why am I Rill — Raye ? "

A little trickle seeking its own larger life; a
little pencil of light sent from a Heart of Light, to
find — to do — to give — something, somewhere!

It flashed upon her suddenly. "Why, I am glad they named me Rill Raye!" she said. "If I am that, I can be content to feel my way awhile!"

It was the first little real gospel that had come to her.

Suddenly, along the path somewhere further on, a child's cry sounded. A broken scream, ejaculations of terror, a shrill command of expostulating fear. "No! no! go — 'way! Get out! Leave me be! Don't! Be still! Oh — h!"

Rill sprang up and hastened forward. Coming around a turn among the trees, she saw, just a few paces ahead, a little girl, one of the farmhouse children, struggling with a strong red Irish setter, which, whether in play or threatening earnest, had got the better of the child, and was overpowering its little strength, leaping upon and pulling her down. The child pushed and screamed, and would hold the creature on the ground for an instant, then trying suddenly to spring from him and run away, would be caught and overset again, the dog tugging with short growling barks at her clothes, and nosing at her feet, his body curving and vibrating from side to side, and his tail flourishing in high excitement. However it began, and however little it really menaced, the poor little maid was completely exhausted.

Rill rushed up and seized the dog by the collar

with both her hands. "Now run!" she cried to
the child, who with her slight remnant of strength
hurried off as best she might toward the open field
beyond which lay the farm buildings; her small
face, still dilated and distorted with the pale horror,
turned back again now and then as she ran, upon
Rill, wrestling in her turn with the lithe, muscular
brute.

And Rill had quite enough of it. There was
more of the growl now than the bark, in such
voice as the dog could make with two hands between his throat and collar; and his eyes looked
dangerous.

How long could Rill hold on? For to let go,
she did not dare. Would the little girl think to
send her any help? Could she drag the creature
out in sight of the houses or of any one who might
perceive and come to her? She shouted in her
turn, but no one seemed to hear. She knew the
picnic people were quite away, upon the other side
of the hill, probably just now gathering around the
tables for their repast.

"Oh, help!" she cried. "Help!" and the dog
sprang under her hands and rolled himself over,
with angry jaws uppermost. She had hard ado
to twist with him and keep her grasp. It was a
battle. There was real peril. The animal was
thoroughly exasperated.

But strong, quick steps came crashing along the woodpath, snapping the fallen stems. A man's voice called out, "Hold fast! I'm coming!" and Dr. Harriman, running at full speed, made a long spring and stood beside her. Now a second pair of hands seized the collar, and Rill's were released.

"Can you go to the house or barn and fetch a piece of rope, or call somebody?"

Rill stopped for no demur or thanks, but sped over the grass, the way the child had gone.

"Common sense!" the doctor articulated, between his shut teeth and deep breaths, admiringly. "I knew it!"

He held the dog with a grip whose force the creature recognized and partially submitted to: the doctor, meanwhile, dragging him along on the way that Rill had taken, so far as the edge of the wood-piece. Here he stopped, beside a strong young ash-tree. In three minutes Rill came flying back again, a tying-rein in one hand, a bit of chain in the other. She had snatched the first things she could lay hands upon, in the nearest barn.

"Good!" Now slip the chain under the collar, between my hands — so. Can you get the strap through the links at the ends? Very well! Dare you try to hold him a minute?"

For answer, Rill put her hands in the place of the doctor's, as he moved first one and then the other. In half a minute more, the strap was made fast round the ash trunk. Then Dr. Harriman relieved Rill again, and bade her retreat. For himself, he gave the dog one strong fling off, and stepped easily to Rill's side.

"Come back into the shade and rest," said he.

CHAPTER XII.

A RESCUE, a defense, anything like this is a most useful element in the resources of fiction; and the reason is, that it is one of the most powerfully operating circumstances in the drawing of any two human natures and lives together, in love or friendship. To owe something of the life, to have been a protection or a saving to it, this, on either part, is a magnetism developed by the act and service in its two quick, mutually urgent, relativities. The power and bestowal; the grateful, glad reception, these are positive and negative to each other at once.

It was with a new personal consciousness and recognition that Dr. Harriman and Rill walked back together into the beautiful seclusion of the pines, and seated themselves under the grand old far-spreading oak. It was a new vitalizing point in their acquaintance with each other, from which might spring and unfold for them a quite new course of sentiment and event.

Rill was feeling this, in an unwonted, restful confidence and a happy admiration that it was satisfying to her nature to be able to render, for full cause, to her companion. Without analysis or question she could, just now, be glad to think so honoringly of Dr. Harriman, so peacefully of herself as in a sure, brave, generous care.

Dr. Harriman was considering the new position, not without a pure, manly pleasure, but as vantage and opportunity also, which he was not quite determined how far to use. He was finding himself to be just a little too much, perhaps, in earnest. He had not meant to be in earnest quite so soon.

With the two, therefore, there was this present difference: the one was moved, surprised with a strange experience, off her guard; the other was moved also, but coolly critical of his emotions, and carefully self-possessed.

" How came you to be here? " Rill asked, in her direct fashion, as she regained breath and quietness, and, with the impulse to say something, shrank somehow from words of thanks. She did not keep back tones, however; they were in her question, they thrilled it with the quick, warm acknowledgment of what it had been to her that he was here.

" As you came to be, I think, Miss Rill. It was still and sweet down here, and I was drawn."

"I was driven," said Rill, concisely.

"Between two forces one cannot always distinguish which chiefly, or most directly, moves," said Dr. Harriman. "But it is a human instinct to invade a peace or pleasantness. I wonder why we can hardly ever make ourselves one with it. Our restlessness breaks up the very calm that it wanted. We cannot get into a solitude after all."

"One human being *is* a population anywhere," assented Rill Raye. "He can't leave his world behind him. Perhaps all we can do is to get now and then into a place where other people's worlds won't crowd ours. And yet, it seems as if in some places our own might stop crowding. I suppose that is the real why of the instinct."

"We make pictures, and try to get into them," said Dr. Harriman. "That is human life."

Rill said nothing.

"When I was a boy," Dr. Harriman began again, "I cried uproariously one day till I half distracted my mother, like Whimpy in the song, because I could n't get into a picture. 'I *will* be a boy in a picture!' I declared. My mother said quietly, 'You *are* a boy in a picture;' and she brought a looking-glass and held it up before me. She did not even ask me if I liked the boy in the picture. She knew where to stop, if I did n't."

"What did you do?" asked Rill.

"I kicked the looking-glass, but I never kicked that boy out of it. I've remembered him ever since; and it has kept me from some impetuous unreasonableness, I think. I may see the pictures and want to be in them; but I do not kick nor scream, and I try not to be in a hurry. I shall get there some time, may be; I mean to; but meanwhile, it's a shifting world, Miss Raye; there are dissolving views!"

Rill's eyes looked intelligent; there was a little mischief in them.

"Meanwhile, one practices tableaux, perhaps?" she said.

"Possibly; one may posture a little; it is instructive. But don't you see how fictitious all that is? One *waits* for the reality."

"Ah!"

"What was that little hard breath for, Miss Raye?"

"For the Lady of Shalott. *Her* mirror cracked from side to side, you know; and all because Sir Lancelot rode by — in a picture."

"Could Sir Lancelot help that, when he was on his way to Camelot?"

"May be not. Camelot was to blame, I suppose. It was Camelot she was forbidden. There are a great many Camelots," said the young girl, gravely.

" I wish I could tell you " — began Dr. Harriman, impulsively. He had risen and stood over her now, looking down at her with an earnestness which perhaps it was as well she did not at the moment see.

She was apparently intent upon a cluster of little wood blossoms that grew in a tuft at her side. She passed her finger up their stems, that rose so daintily out from their rich, low leafage. There was a curious tenderness in her touch as it stroked the delicate petals upward. It was as if she felt with them somewhat of their lowly, hidden, unsought life.

Dr. Harriman interrupted himself, noting the action which, perhaps, afforded him a timely relief from an imprudence he was nearly uttering.

" You do not gather the flowers, Miss Rill ? " he said, with an inflection as if he asked her why.

" No. I have n't that propensity. I think it is the same which makes men shoot birds. I like live flowers — growing. I don't care for corpses of flowers." Her eyes flashed upward at him as she spoke. It was one of her quaint, queer speeches which, nevertheless, she meant, while she smiled at her own queerness that often seemed to surprise herself when she had uttered it.

There was something irresistible in her; in her originality, her genuineness; the sparkling up of the life in her, like the rush and shine of a clear water-spring. It was a nature to study with delight. To have a claim to study it, to sympathize with it — this suddenly, and not for the first time, drew Dr. Harriman with a keen desire.

He sat down again, a little way off, opposite her, upon an old fallen log. His feet rested in a bed of wintergreen. He pulled a stem of it, and rubbed the fragrant leaves in his fingers; his arms resting upon his knees as he bent forward, his head down a little in a pause of thoughtfulness.

"May I tell you something of my life?" he asked Rill Raye.

Rill Raye herself was being drawn; in spite of a strange feeling that it was not a true drawing, that it was only of the moment, she was yielding to a new sense of liking for this man, who was showing himself to her in new lights. She was stirred; she was a little frightened. What could he be going to say, and why did he want to say it? Did she really want to hear? She was not sure; yet she could not speak the word to stop him.

So, with her silence for assent, Dr. Harriman began and told her the things of which we already know. Of what the motive had been thus far in his life, and what it must be for a while longer; of his duties, that he did not mean selfishly to set aside; of hopes that a man must have, which he

had not been free to indulge. He acknowledged
that, with these hindrances, he had been wrong,
perhaps, in things that she had noticed and had
bravely charged him with. He thanked her for her
true speaking; it made an opportunity for him to
speak frankly in return, and he wished very much
that she should understand him.

"I cannot bear," he said, "that you should think
me a mere flirt. That is such an odious name for
a man. It has in it a woman's foolish vanity, and
a man's culpable deceit. I am not a flirt. Miss
Raye. I may have trifled, when trifling was all
that was expected, or returned; one does feel the
difference, Miss Rill; but when I am in earnest, it
will be — if I can make her listen — with a woman
who will not flirt."

I do not think Dr. Harriman deliberately borrowed his phrase from Putnam King. It had
struck him at the time, and it came to him now as
the natural word for his own meaning. We say a
good many things so, perhaps even without recol-
lecting; there is a good deal of verbal plagiarism.
Indeed, it makes language: out of it proverbs
grow; we do not know where they first came from.
But Dr. Harriman colored a little, remembering,
as the words came to his lips, how they had been
said to him.

Rill Raye had lifted up her head and was look-

ing at him with full, clear eyes. They were eyes
that saw beyond the surface, as they were themselves not surface eyes, but took their color and
their gleam from depth. Her look was of a listening that sounded down beneath his word. It found
something there which he had not meant to express — to the ear, at any rate. It was not of the
ear's hearing. A color came into the girl's face
too ; not of embarrassment, or shy feeling, or any
timid consciousness such as he might have been
pleased to see there, and half dismayed to have so
soon evoked with but his half intent. It was a
rising of some womanly resentment that waited,
not quite certain of offense.

"I do not think you are quite frank with me,
even yet, Dr. Harriman," she said, with the directness that was in her eyes. "I do not quite know
why you say — why you need to say — these things
to me at all."

A coquettish woman — leading him on — might
have spoken these very words ; but not as Rill
Raye spoke them. There was a demand in them ;
there was a rebuke, if he deserved it. If he had
known all that was moving her to say them, he
might not have been disconcerted as he was. But
how could he suspect that this Rill Raye, who had
learned of things that made her look back with an
honest self-scorn upon her own little sillinesses and

mistakes of awhile ago, was not even sure that he did not mean what would include herself among such girls as had been willing to trifle and put themselves in the way of being trifled with, — girls from whom he would never choose the woman he should come to in manly earnest? How could he guess that through her mind was rushing at this instant the swift suspicion of his having heard the miserable word of gossip that had come round to her, — that she might choose between two men, neither of whom had given her the least sign? " Does he suppose I thought so, — that perhaps I said so?" she was wondering, with a pang of wrath and shame, kept down only by the strong determination to make certain before she would give way to it. Why had he come near her at all with his friendliness, as he unquestionably had done lately more and more, if this were what he could think of her?

He had treated her as if he had learned respect for her ; as if he cared for her opinion. For this very reason, would he be so bitterly honest with her as this? Honest? No; he was not absolutely honest, as she said to him. Was he just kind enough to let her know, for her own sake, how he stood, while veiling his explanation with the pretense of seeking to make her understand what he had not intended elsewhere?

She waited, to be sure of this; an instant more, and the startled flush would be a scorch of indignation. He had no right; she had done nothing to give him right or provocation. She might scorn herself; but he need not scorn her. She looked at him with that steady, searching demand in her face.

He lost his presence of mind before it; he was self-convicted of his own unworthy half-dealing. He spoke as a man who must say something, but who is not ready with the thing to say, and blurts forth that which he would not have said at all.

"Because, Miss Raye — because — I wanted you to know my position. To understand — that there might be other things — different things — that I could not say."

Then the eyes flashed, and the color deepened. She looked as she had looked that day when she had demanded and borne a pain that might buy back her dignity.

"Since you thought it necessary — since you were under such a mistake, Dr. Harriman," she said, slowly, "I am glad you did it. I am able to answer you. It was *not* necessary at all; and being unnecessary, it was " —

There she stopped. He had just done her a service; she would not tell him that he had offered her an impertinence. She must endure her obligation to him ; she must thank him for that, at least. Her anger took a touch of gentler pain. She had begun really to like him — to be glad of his esteem.

She had risen to her feet. This compelled him to rise also. She held out her hand to him. " I owe you for a great service," she said. " I do not forget that. Perhaps you have heard the same meddling story that I have ; perhaps you thought I believed it. I dare say you only meant to be kind, but you have been altogether mistaken, and you have offended me ; if I were not offended, I should deserve it all. Good-by ! " She turned round, away from him, and walked down the little foot-track among the leaves.

"Miss Raye ! Where are you going ? Do not leave me like this ! Forgive me ! I did not mean one word of what you think ! "

He followed her ; she paused and looked back at him.

" Please, Dr. Harriman, let me go," she said. " We have been long enough away from the others. I wish you would go back to them. I do not mean to ; I am tired. They will let me rest there at the farmhouse ; then I shall go home. Perhaps you will find my aunt for me and tell her."

She gave him thus much of forgiveness — that he might do her this little service more. She walked on ; it was impossible that he should persist, and dog her steps. He lifted his hat with some word of strong regret, and of " another time ; " then he took his way as she had bidden him, a man with a quite new experience in his life.

How would she get home ? He had not asked her this ; in the face of her simple determination it had not occurred to him any more than if she had been a creature with wings. It occurred to him now ; but he dared not go back to her. He might — if he had not been a fool — have driven her home himself. His horse and phaeton were at the farmhouse stables. He might have had that lovely ride with her, back through the long pine woods. He might have said something very different from the thing he had said. She was a woman worth waiting for ; a woman who would have known how to wait, if it had been with, not for, a man.

One of those stupidities in life had happened by which the whole current of events had been changed, and to his bitter loss. Could he ever, by any happier chance, retrieve it? *Could* he? He would. He would not question, he would make chance ; he would redeem himself ; he would marry Rill Raye yet.

No sooner had he disappeared among the trees, and Rill, with furtive glances, had made sure of it, than she sat down again upon the nearest resting-place, a stone at the wood-edge. She was in need of at least a momentary repose, and the need asserted itself suddenly. She was pale and exhausted, almost faint, as the tension of her spirit relaxed. What she would have liked was a good cry; but she dared not take it here; and a cry can wait, though at some expense of nerve. A little way off, the dog still tugged at his strong fastening, and barked and growled. This did not help to calm her, though she knew he could not get away. Why did not the farm people hear him, and come? She began to pity the poor creature. Things were hard in this world for all sorts of struggling, halfway natures.

An easy-rolling carriage came along over the turf and the pine needles of the roadway. Mrs. Rextell's pretty victoria, with herself and Mrs. Sholto for occupants. Rill stood up as it approached. Mrs. Rextell leaned forward to the coachman with a word, and the carriage stopped.

"My dear! what is it?" asked the lady. "You are alone; you look pale; has anything happened?"

"I have been frightened by the dog: Dr. Harriman came and helped me, and tied him to the tree. I am going to the farmhouse to tell them; then I shall go home."

" But how ? — excuse me."

" I don't know.   Somebody will take me, I suppose."   And then, — to the remaining question in
Mrs. Rextell's eyes which took a shade of surprise, — " aunt Amelia will know.   Dr. Harriman
has gone to tell her," she said, simply.

" My dear," said Mrs. Rextell, quickly, " you
are not fit to stand to say another word.   I will
tell you what to do.   Keep on to the farmhouse,
and wait there ; I am only going to the grounds
for a few minutes, to speak to one or two people,
and leave Mrs. Sholto.   I will see Miss Bonable
myself.   Then I will come back for you, and we
will drive home together.   Shall we ? "

" You are very kind," said Rill.   " I shall be
glad."

Mrs. Rextell's face lighted with approving satisfaction.   The girl had not hesitated.   " Drive on,
Sandis," she ordered, and nodded with a smile to
Cyrilla, to leave whom at once was now the greater
kindness.   " Look for Miss Bonable as you come
up to the party, and bring me as near to her as
you can," she added to her servant.   " I will re-
lieve Dr. Harriman of the remainder of this business," she thought to herself as she settled back
against the cushions.

The ladies overtook Dr. Harriman on the way,
and passed him with a polite exchange of bows.

Miss Bonable was quickly found, and Mrs. Rextell and her friend alighted. As they crossed the few steps from the roadway into the little glade between rocks and trees where the supper party still lingered, a new thought came to Mrs. Rextell. " Shall you have a spare seat ? " she asked Mrs. Sholto. " How is Colonel Sholto coming ? "

" In the landau. Oh, yes ; Jack will ride ! "

Dr. Harriman came up from a cross path in time to see Miss Bonable seated in the Rextell victoria, and turning out upon the drive. Mrs. Rextell met him. " I saw Miss Raye," she told him, " as I came in. I have sent Miss Bonable to her. What was the matter with the dog ? "

She spoke in very friendly fashion. Dr. Harriman answered her categorically. " Thank you ; that was the best thing," he said. " There was nothing really the matter ; the dog was frolicsome and rude ; he frightened a little girl ; Miss Raye went to the rescue, and she had her hands full. It did become a little serious at last ; those Irish setters are uncertain, and the fellow had his temper up."

" And you came along just in time ? " the lady queried, pleasantly. If there were any meaning in her question it did not appear, either on her side, or in his reception of it.

" None too soon for Miss Raye's strength, I

think," he answered; and lifting his hat toward his head with a deference, he replaced it, and moved from her as Mrs. Sholto rejoined her friend.

There was a subdued gravity about the gentleman which impressed Mrs. Rextell. "Something has happened," she said to herself, while she spoke a few quite other words to Mrs. Sholto. "I don't believe *he* was frightened. I wonder if Rill Raye can have refused him!"

The victoria came round to the farmhouse door, with Miss Bonable very upright in it, as if at once careful of undue freedom with a borrowed splendor, and none the less entirely equal to the occasion.

Rill came out, surprised.

"Well, are you ready to go home?" Miss Bonable inquired, with a manner of course. Rill replied by entering the low vehicle. "All right," said Miss Bonable to the inflexible Sandis, who sat like a statue, or a cataleptic. "I don't suppose he would turn round, if we were both to tumble out behind," aunt Amelia remarked, in a tone withdrawn to the interior. This was a graciousness, as taking Rill into some sympathy and companionship. The girl had expected either silence or stern catechising.

But aunt Amelia did not catechise. For one reason, Sandis was trained to hear with the back of his ears. They rolled smoothly along through the deep, fragrant pine wood shadow, out upon the North Road, and round to Brook Lane and the cottage.

Miss Bonable told Sandis that she was very much obliged. She might as well have told the Sphinx. His impassive eyes were upon his horse's ears, his profile was a fixed, stately line ; he made some mysterious, magnetic sign, without sound or apparent motion, and the victoria rolled away.

Perhaps the vexation of her superfluous thanks was in the single sentence which she addressed to Rill as they went upstairs.

" You have a faculty for getting into scrapes ; and for everybody knowing it," she said. " I wonder what will happen next ! "

But there was no scathe nor scorn in her tone. Whatever her words were, this was gentleness for Miss Bonable. It had not been altogether a scrape, since Mrs. Rextell had lent her countenance — and her carriage — to the emergency. Miss Bonable might not submit to hash parties, but she valued private and individual attentions.

There was more than this in her forbearance, however. She had not found it to be of much use to scold or accuse Cyrilla, and she had learned, through Miss Haven's sympathetic influence, some wiser reliefs.

CHAPTER XIII.

"THAT'S WHAT I'M A SPINSTER FOR."

THE next day Miss Bonable was restless. She would like to see Miss Haven. But that lady not being at home, she called, on her way from the Point, to see cousin Sarah. She not only felt that she must speak to somebody herself, but she foresaw there would be "talk" about this matter, as about all matters, in Wewachet; and she had found out both the prairie strategy of setting a fire before a fire, and the best place to do it in. So she came into the southwest room with her light parcels of niceties from the grocer, and her purchases from Scrimple. She laid them down beside her on the sofa, and unrolled her little home packet, the story of the day before.

"It would n't have happened to anybody but Rill Raye!" she ended, impatiently.

"I think 's likely 's not," returned Miss Crooke, calmly. "The' ain't many like Rill, Miss Bonable. I hope you 're proud of her."

"I know you stand her friend; and that 's why

I speak about it. But I don't see why she was down there anyway."

"I don't see why you expect to see everything, specially things that ain't there," said Miss Crooke. Her sharp sententiousness was a comfort to Miss Bonable, whether meant to be or not. She went on with her grievance, perhaps to get more comfort.

"There'll be a buzz about it. They'll say it was a contrivance to meet Dr. Harriman."

"Or the dog," put in Miss Sarah.

Miss Bonable could not resist a smile. It was a pity she ever could. When she showed her beautiful, even teeth, set in their peculiar, delicate oval, and her eyes relaxed their searchingness and let the light through them, she was for the moment a fair, sweet-faced woman, — the woman she had been before eye and lip grew hard.

"She'll get talked of again, that's all; it's her way, and her luck," she said.

"There's more 'n one way of talkin'," said Sarah Crooke, "and the more 's really known about some folks, the better. But don't *you* talk, — don't *you* buzz, Amelia Bonable! I'm pleased you've come to me with it; but you just drop it right here, and leave it, — will you?"

Miss Amelia's eyes opened wide. "I — talk! about Cyrilla!"

"Yes, you. You don't do it abroad; it's new for you to come here; but you talk at home — to her — and to yourself. That's where it begins. That's what puts things in the air. If they're in the closet, they're out on the housetop. That's Scripture, and its experience. If you don't want a thing to circulate, don't turn it round in your own mind. It's like a tornado; if it once gets a-whirlin', it'll start off. What worries and twists in a little back corner of your own thoughts, is down-street making a dust before you know it. It's the rule of things. What you would n't like other folks to mistrust, don't you mistrust."

Miss Bonable went home with a fresh kink in her philosophy.

Miss Haven came back, a few days later, from Newport, and cousin Sarah told her all about it. "I declare," she said, "that woman — Amelia Bonable — makes me feel feeble. I don't know what to say to her. She ain't bad — nor bad-hearted; but she endures a lot of trouble beforehand. If folks will set on misery's eggs, they need n't complain when something hatches!"

Miss Haven laughed. The next day she began her little rounds again in Wewachet. "There is always something to fetch and to carry," said the barefaced newsmonger.

She made half a dozen calls; she wanted to know

everything that had happened while she had been away. She gathered and distributed; she went armed and equipped from one house to the next; she became utterance and authority; she mixed herself with what she heard, and characterized it. The bended bow and the voice passed on, and it was generous good-will that the message carried.

All was of interest; all was discussed: from Edith Pinceley's new gown, that she "suspected was a quiet present — from Mrs. Sholto, perhaps; Edith was a good deal there " — to the incidents and adventures at Shepaug; Connie Norris's sauciness, and George Craigan's manly facing of it — " It will do them both good," Miss Haven said; " they will understand each other yet; there is a fair making in both of them " — to Rill and the little farmhouse girl, the fright and the bravery, and Mrs. Rextell. Dr. Harriman was slipped back into a second place. " Oh, yes, he helped Rill tie up the dog," was all he got of comment or applause.

" Mrs. Rextell is growing very fond of Rill, I think, and she has an especially great respect for Miss Bonable. It is nice for them all. You are such very friendly people here, Mrs. Rospey," said the dear Machiavel, in her last twilight call.

" It 's you that have done it. It 's a neighborhood now — or the beginning of one; and it never was before you came. You've spun us together, somehow."

Elizabeth Haven did not contradict; she knew it was true. "That's what I'm a spinster for," she said, lightly, with the tears in her eyes; and in her heart she thanked the Lord.

She had woven her sunshine in very small threads; she was content to drop tiny, patient dews of speech; only once in a while, upon occasion, she came down here or there with some full blaze of a reserved knowledge, some shower of generous surprise, that made suddenly a spring day and a greenness of new blades where else might have been a lingering of frost and winterkill.

One autumn day, later on, she was sitting with Mrs. Rextell in her little conservatory parlor. A wide window looked into depths of firs and larches, up and down whose branching slopes ran pretty cedar birds. A glass door was open upon sheltered loveliness of ferns and roses, heliotropes and carnations, budding lilies. The air was full of delicate fragrances, with sunbeams filtering softly through. It was a fit place for two sweet, sunny-hearted women to sit and talk together.

Mrs. Sholto had just gone out.

"Isn't she lovely?" said Mrs. Rextell, coming back to her chair beside Miss Haven, after parting from her other visitor at the door. "Nobody half knew her before her second marriage. How should they, when hardly half of her had chance to be alive? How strange it is, this taking people for granted at their weak exceptions and passing disadvantages, and sending them on labeled with the record! I do hate talk about one's neighbors. And a little place like this is full of it."

"Not half so full as it ought to be. People don't tell half the *good* news. If they only knew what they are doing with their showing-up and stigmatizing the wrong, untrue thing; the thing, may be, a soul is going to the Lord with in sore trouble! It is making spectacle of mortal pain!"

"It is worse; it is *making* the mortal pain. It is vivisection," said Mrs. Rextell, indignantly.

By unspoken suggestion, they went on from that — these two so little lower than the angels — with tender mentions that were healings, or inquiries that sought healings. Presently, their speech turned upon Rill Raye and Miss Bonable. No; talk does not turn itself; Miss Haven turned it.

"Miss Bonable is a person one can hardly ever accomplish an intention with," said Mrs. Rextell. "It is a pity; it is a hindrance to Miss Raye."

"Do you think it is so hard?"

"Yes, usually; if you do accomplish anything, it stands by itself. You cannot begin again where you left off." She was thinking of Shepaug, and of certain little failures afterward to follow up her own advance there; failures due, really, to Miss Bonable's stern determination not to seem to expect the ell from the inch. "She is exceedingly blunt," said Mrs. Rextell.

"Exceedingly," said Miss Haven. "Therefore, one must not try to get round her bluntness with any ordinary — or extraordinary — suavity. One must go very straight to the point, facing her own honesty."

"Perhaps so; and very deep, too. She is not to be met on the surface. Maybe I should have said one cannot accomplish with her an *at*tention. It is of no use to invite her, for instance."

"No; not as a matter of course. She says she will not go to hash parties."

Mrs. Rextell laughed merrily. "Is that what she calls my neighborhood entertainments? It's capital! I never should have had the wit to think of it. I'm sure I never had the deliberate meaning in the thing; but it is just what they are — and everybody's else — the big, general ones. I suppose it is a natural variation from 'first chop!' I never thought what that meant before!"

There is an indescribable delicate touch that a high-bred person can give to a phrase of slang, just glancing at it with piquant quotation. The

words fell from Mrs. Rextell's lips with a grace of
dainty strangeness.

"I certainly do respect Miss Bonable," she went
on, brightly. "I always thought her really excellent, but with odd, rough ways that rather turn
aside approach, you know. That is hard for her
niece. Miss Raye is charming, — only, just a little
— emphasized? Some people seem to be printed
in italics; I suppose they cannot help it ; but one
hardly prefers the type — for a young girl?"
Mrs. Rextell spoke with gentle rising inflections,
putting things with interrogation.

"May be not, if the type be coarse, or an ex-
aggeration. But a uniform, delicate script, only
unusual for its clearness and grace, and the text
something worthy a special setting?" Miss Haven
replied with similar fine query.

"That is what you think? I am glad, and thank
you. But, — again, — is n't there some misreading
there — on both sides, perhaps? Don't they —
rather — put each other in a bad light? I wish, —
it is because I feel, somehow, interested in both,
I don't know why, — I wish I could understand."

"I think it would be good you should understand," said Miss Haven to that, with a sudden
decision. "I will tell you the whole story."

And then the golden gossip took on her what
only a golden gossip can, who discerns with heavenly

freemasonry and speaks in love. In ten minutes more Mrs. Rextell knew, of this inner human history, what the ministering spirits knew, and took it into the same pure keeping.

When Miss Haven had finished, her auditor sat silent a moment,· folding it away. "And that," she said, presently, with a tender reverence in her voice, " is "—

" That is Miss Bonable," replied Miss Haven, to her pause. " She is stiff and gnarled, perhaps, but she is "—

" She is a cedar of Lebanon," interrupted Mrs. Rextell.

Miss Haven left that unanswered.

Mrs. Rextell came to the end of her dark-olive wool, and searched in her basket for some soft canary. "And the girl knows nothing of all this?" she asked, as she joined on the beautiful contrast.

" Nothing; further than that she 'lost' her mother when she was little, and that her father went away and never came back again, and so she came to belong to aunt Amelia."

" And never did belong. There should not have been so much hiding. At any rate she is old enough now to know more."

" But how could Miss Bonable ever tell her? How could she tell her enough for her really to understand ? The two things that were the signifi-

cance of it all — her father's fickleness and her
mother's shame — she could not tell her those!"

"I don't know. Perhaps not all at once, or at
the first. But little by little, as came natural, as
she would surely ask. Oh, there is always a way
to tell the truth ; or else it takes a way to tell itself!
That child has lived in the dark, Miss Haven."

"It is a reason — I have felt so — why we should
help her up into the light."

"But the man — the father; why has he done
nothing at his end ? Why has he been content ?"
Mrs. Rextell was warmly roused. Her beautiful
eyes shone ; her color was fervent; she leaned
toward her friend, dropping her work, a confusion
of soft brilliancy, upon her lap.

"I suppose he had little hope for the child of
such mothering; except as he could leave her,
without interference, to the different one. I suppose he was discouraged, disgusted, at first ; then
— away out there, and busy with a man's work —
he grew indifferent, and forgot, almost. Men do ;
they are not like women. He never forgot his duty
about her, it seems, however ; he has sent money,
year by year, to Miss Bonable."

"More than her mere support, I wonder ?"

"I think so. Miss Bonable says he has 'done
well enough' out there. She has taken care of
whatever came, so that it should be safe for Cyrilla

by and by. It has not been used for her support."

"And Cyrilla has known nothing about that, either, I dare say."

"There was no need yet; Miss Bonable thought better not. She gives her every six months the rent of the little place at Maplefield, which Rill knows she owns. That makes a fair allowance for her, and affords her the experience of taking care of money; which Miss Bonable says a girl can learn as well with ten dollars as with a hundred. 'If you can hem a towel, you can hem a sheet,' she says."

"But it won't be fair to her, very long. She ought to know what she can do in the world. And — why, it's keeping her out of all her birthrights, Miss Haven! She has a right to her father; to her child's love and duty; she has a right to the debt of gratitude and honor she owes her aunt. It ought not to go on so!"

"I have said all that to Miss Bonable, but she puts it off. 'What would come of it?' she asks. She could not send Rill over to that other end of the world; and she could not ask Rill's father to come here. I suppose those two have been separately and tacitly agreed that it was better to have the half circumference of the earth between them."

"Is the other woman living?"

" I think Miss Bonable hardly knows. There was a name among the death notices in a paper once, that might have been the one she would have called herself by ; but Miss Bonable never learned anything more. Very possibly it was only a coincidence. What inclines me to think that Mr. Raye may have kept some trace of her, and know that she is still living, is the fact that he does not come back."

" I see ; but suppose Miss Bonable should die ? "

" She has provided that he shall know, in that case. ' It will not be far — for him — then,' she said."

" I don't believe it is all the way round, with either of them, now," said imaginative Mrs. Rextell. " There are straight lines that tie the ends of the widest arcs."

" Yes ; there are other axes than the one from pole to pole. Lives turn upon many such."

" And Miss Bonable cannot be much above forty, now. A fresh, fair woman, too — when you look at her in the light that belongs to her. Well, one cannot meddle with *that*, even in wishing. But the other things — that father and daughter should not know each other all these years ; that they should be suddenly thrust together some time, perhaps, not the least prepared what to make of each other ; that he should be thinking of her with all the pos-

sibility in her of that other parentage, and losing
sight of her as his own child ; that while she is turning out — who knows how, with such repression —
he should not know her real sweetness and strength
and promise — and, oh, her need ! If somebody
could only write to him and tell him *that*, Miss
Haven ! "

" I have written," said Miss Haven quietly.

CHAPTER XIV.

Miss Bonable's white front gate swung upon its hinges, and Mrs. Rextell came up the grass walk. Miss Bonable saw her from an upper window. If the lady had come in her carriage, I doubt if she would have been let in. In her morning dress, with a shawl and parasol, she had just walked over, not like a caller, but like a neighbor. Clementhy Pond was in the kitchen, scalding pickles: Miss Bonable came down the front stairs and unlatched the blinds, behind which the door stood open. The day was one of summer warmth.

"Thank you," said Mrs. Rextell, holding out her hand. "May I came in?"

"If you please," Miss Bonable answered, mildly, with civil response of hand-greeting, but no effusion. "But Cyrilla is out."

"I came to see you," replied her visitor. "It is early, and I should apologize. But I wanted to be sure to find you."

Miss Bonable led the way into the parlor, and

put forward a comfortable cushioned chair, seating
herself on one of the prim old-fashioned six of her
original furnishing. She waited her guest's word,
her pleasure, or the errand of her visit, not offering
any initial remark, and leaving the undeniable
weather to its own demonstration. Mrs. Rextell
had come for something, probably, beyond the seeing her in her morning gown, which was of homely
brown calico, while the other lady wore a fabrica-
tion of soft silk and wool, as plain and modest as
need be, yet with no suggestion of any coarse or
common use.

Mrs. Rextell met the composure of Miss Bonable's silence with equal composure of pleasant,
ready speech. "I found this little wild rose in the
lane," she said, holding out a pink blossom with a
lovely carmine depth at the heart, against which
golden stamens rested. "See how bright it is, and
so curiously shaded. One does not look for roses
and autumn leaves together. But they are exquisite in contrast," and she laid the rose's cheek
against the glossy bronze of a bit of bramble.

"Colors are all brighter in the fall," said Miss
Bonable, "even when things are blooming out of
season. Wild roses are queer; they come most
any time, in some places."

"The goldenrod was dazzling all along," said
Mrs. Rextell. "But after I found this, I thought

I would go home with only my one little wild rose.
Miss Bonable, I want to get you to come and see
me. I would like you to bring Miss Raye; but
I want you at any rate. That is what I came to
say this morning. Will you take tea with me on
Thursday?"

"I thank you, Mrs. Rextell; I don't believe I
can," answered Miss Bonable, bluntly.

"Mrs. Sholto and Miss Haven will be there, —
only those," persisted Mrs. Rextell, sweetly. She
would not ask Miss Bonable and Rill quite by
themselves; that, again, is only a compliment
where intimacy is established. You can take anybody in, on special basis; that is as indiscriminate
as a hash party. But one or two — to meet one or
two — chosen, as these were; this was what expressed precisely Mrs. Rextell's intent.

"I know you don't like large companies; one
never really sees people so; they are only what
must be once in a while, as we have thunderstorms,
to restore equilibrium."

Miss Bonable colored up with sudden consciousness. But her eyes were clear and steady enough.
"Did Elizabeth Haven tell you that?" she demanded, looking full in her interlocutor's face.

"My dear Miss Bonable — what?"

"I am sure she did. What I said about the
hash parties."

Mrs. Rextell laughed; that sweet ring of a laugh that was peculiarly hers. " You were quite right. It was the best thing anybody has said for ever so long. But that is n't why I want you now."

" Elizabeth Haven is a tattler."

" I believe she is ; and I believe we both like her the better for it. Won't you come ? "

" I 'm a very plain person, Mrs. Rextell. And I 'm hard."

" You are hard to invite, certainly." She was still smiling; her look was both amused and warm; she was longing to draw to herself this plain, hard person, in whom she found such element of worth.

" I 'm hard, and I 'm rough ; I 'm not like you ; it 's too late for me to be that now," Miss Bonable said. " I might have been — if things had begun at the beginning. There 's a sweet spot in me ; but I 've had to shut myself up over it." All her face had softened, quickly ; the truth of the moment got spoken, as it always did with her ; and at this moment it was the truth she hid for the most part even from herself. Her eyes had lost their sharpness ; they were limpid and intent; her lips took that gentle curve which showed their shape of youth ; the white arch of the teeth broke from between them.

Mrs. Rextell rose from her seat, and came over to her. " Some things are so rich, so precious, that they need putting in safe, hard cases," she said. "The milk in the nut would be wasted, but for the burr. But, when the time comes, the burr opens, my dear friend; and we gather the ripe sweetness." She put out both her hands, now; the little wild rose in one of them fell to the floor. "You will come and take tea with me?" she repeated.

"It is you that will, I think. Yes; I suppose I must, this time." But the two hands were taken; and a thrill came through them from the sweet woman - heart whence they were stretched out, that found and touched the other behind its life-shell.

Mrs. Rextell was gone; Miss Bonable stood alone; she said to herself, "I suppose I've been a fool; I am, generally, one way or another. I could n't seem to help it, though; it was as if she must know everything."

She picked up the wild rose, and carried it away with her upstairs. She went to her bureau drawers; she looked up some fine old laces; she unwrapped from silver paper a little white shawl, with mystic threads stitched into it upon one end; she laid these things together upon the black silk dress folded long by itself below. She shut the drawers, and went downstairs, with a smile half pleasure, half amused self-tolerance. She took hold vigorously with Clementhy Pond upon the pickle-work; she did up a lot of barberries and sweet apples; she scalded her spiced-currant; the two women accomplished a vast piece of housewifely business that day. They stood for hours on the cold brick buttery floor, wiping shelves and jars, filling and ranging. It was a goodly show.

But on the Wednesday Miss Bonable was in her bed, full of pain and fever. It was the beginning of a long illness. The black silk, and the white camel's-hair, and the old lace, lay quietly together for weeks and weeks.

CHAPTER XV.

BREAKS AND JOINS.

THINGS hardly ever join on, after an interruption, to be as they were before the break. You go away from home leaving matters in a certain relative position upon which you calculate for continuance with some postponed purpose. You come back to find everything *chasséed* into fresh combination ; some things out of question that were in important bearing before ; some old hindrance nonexistent, may be, but new difficulty and obstacle in the way ; your world upheaved and tossed about; its face changed by a circumstantial earthquake. In yourself, even, there are altered conditions ; you need a pause before you can see where to begin again ; perhaps whether you may begin at all.

When Putnam King returned to Wewachet, making one of his stops there which had always been brief, but the chain of whose frequency during the past summer had joined them with a practical continuousness, he came into some such altered surroundings, and with a very considerable difference of opportunity. His time was really limited, now; the repetitions of his comings were uncertain. He was expected at Huxtable for a solid family visit, before he should settle down to the grind of the law office. By and by this would hold him close; a great case was coming on this winter, involving the looking up of documents and records, and obtaining of evidence at a distance, which Mr. Arbicon had signified he should depute to him. These things were in the young man's mind; they would prevent, he knew, such easy, natural following to conclusion of his interest and association here as had seemed possible a little while ago, and would force the alternative of long delay and abeyance or very direct and obvious action.

When he found added to all this the complete shifting of centres in the little neighborhood, it was as if he had been blindfolded and turned round three times in the old game, and bidden suddenly to go forward again, with " touch whom you may!"

He could scarcely touch anybody. Aunt Elizabeth was off half her time at the cottage on the North Road; Cyrilla was shut up there with Miss Bonable. Miss Bonable had become, in her sickroom, the focus of attention and regard. Instead of little teas in Miss Haven's library, there were only momentary encounters of ones or twos in Brook Lane and in the cottage parlor, or more established visiting in the off-room upstairs, where Miss Haven or Mrs. Rospey sat with Cyrilla in the hours when she simply had to be within hearing and call, while Miss Amelia rested.

Mrs. Rextell and Mrs. Sholto and Mrs. Vance called frequently; Brook Lane was dinted in the middle with high-bred hoof-tracks, and scored marginally with light wheel-marks, like crimped gingerbread. Fruits and flowers were heaped in parlor and pantry, — great purple-black grapes; golden pears of name and pedigree, each laid separately, like a jewel of amber, on soft white paper or fleecy cotton ; roses and heliotropes and azaleas filling vase and bowl; the fragrance of them all came forth and met you at the door. All this converged here suddenly, and showered down around Miss Amelia Bonable, and into her hard, restrained life. She could not take to herself the half in food or perfume or beauty ; but the loveliness and odor and nourishing of it crept into her heart that had been so lonely. It was a sweeter face that looked up from the pillows ; it was a gentler tone and gesture that answered inquiry or offering.

Dr. Harriman sent quail and pigeons ; she did not half like that, but she only told Rill not to let him do it again ; she was getting not to need such things, and there were plenty of *poor* sick folks in Wewachet, if he wanted to do kindness. So Rill saw him when he came again, and thanked him, telling him that aunt Amelia said he was very good, but begged him not to trouble himself for her any more, as she was getting now to crave the homely, substantial things that were really best for her.

Dr. Harriman took whatever there was of rebuff in this with complacence; Rill had at least been obliged to see him, to bring the message. But, if he gained that, it was all he gained, and the satisfaction did not last him long. She gave him the brief word and excused herself; and he did not see her again, though he called several times.

Putnam King made his little offerings, also; but he came and went with but very unsatisfactory glimpses of even his aunt Elizabeth; and at the cottage he made no attempt, of course, in the present state of things, to go farther than the door. The whole house was upstairs; the women-friends went there; nobody came down, and he could not ask it. Then the weeks at Huxtable intervened, and although he managed to run out to Wewachet the very day he came up from the Cape, he only found a yet more settled withdrawal and isolation barring him off. The little attentions at the door, of inquiry or gift, were neither needed nor plausible now; Miss Bonable was getting well; but it was the slow tediousness of creeping back from positive illness to the taking up of the habits of life again;

and Rill was almost more shut in than before.
This, it was to be suspected, was partly voluntary;
for some reason she did not care to emerge much
from her seclusion; but she was really wanted in
a hundred ways, and at any possible minute. Miss
Bonable had her little invalid occupations, her knitting, her rug work; and Rill waited upon her with
all her furnishings and changes, with handling and
help. She read aloud to her; she arranged her
tray when her food was brought up; she made her
toilets for her; these things took all her time.

If ever a young fellow fell in love, like Prince
Ahmed, through hearsay and from a picture, Put-
man King was getting bewitched in that fashion
with his Aldegonda, now. Aunt Elizabeth was as
simple and clear as a sunbeam; she revealed that
which she shone upon in reflected lights; Putnam
King had only to spring his little kodak upon her
with question or remark, and get a clear impression
of a quiet interior, with Rill Raye as central figure,
in her grace of steadfast self-denial, her royal
womanliness of ministry. He was not barred out,
— he was admitted intimately, to privilege and understanding; to a growing absorption in one sweet,
admiring study. He was learning her now, "in
her natural relations;" as he had said a man must
learn the woman he would care for.

And Rill Raye was unconscious. She was abid-

ing in that foregone conclusion that she had no
dear, real, beautiful, natural surroundings to be
known in ; that hers — and her use of them —
were all against her ; that she could never be
known in herself, for what she was really worth,
by those she would care should know her.

Putnam King had gone away, — had stayed away,
— was never coming any more as he had come.
He had heard that silly, vain story which told as
if it must have set forth from herself, or from near
her, — that of the two she could have her choice.
He had not done as the other did, — " explained "
— that he could not seek or marry her ! He had
not put her to that blush, that indignity. But he
had quietly dropped himself out; there would be
nothing more of Putnam King in her story. There
never *had* been anything ! She had not been a
fool, though he might be afraid of her as one.

There was nothing now for her to do but to take
care of aunt Amelia, and let her own dull life run
on. She thought it would be dull ; that it would
not even be tempestuous with its little bursts of
passion, as it had been. Partly, she did not care ;
and partly, she meant to be more good ; she would
learn patience ; that was what would have to take
the place of pleasure for her, all her years.

Underneath all, a little spring of hidden life —
of possible joy that should, some time, well up

from deeper than all this — made itself conscious in her. She did not quite forget that moment in the lovely, lonely wood; the word that had come to her there: " I have called thee by thy name; thou art mine. Fear not; I have redeemed thee."

Some One was doing something with her, doubtless ; if she could wait and bear, the blind trickling of her hindered life-seeking might come forth from the dark rock cranny and the wilderness tangle, into some fairer, open reach, and find its growth and form ; the little quiver of light that struggled in her might pierce its way across her present darkness, and carry itself — urged by the great pulsing glory out of which it had been born — to the beauty whither it was sent. Cyrilla was very thoughtful in these days ; it seemed, perhaps, to Miss Bonable as if she were only quenched and dulled ; as if she found things very weariful. It was harder now to understand the girl than it had ever been ; aunt Amelia had not thought such mood as this was in her.

Upon Cyrilla's side there was a difference ; she was, in one way, nearer understanding her aunt than she had ever been ; though she also wondered at this new phase in which she saw her. She perceived now through other eyes ; she found out what Miss Bonable could be to those whom she trusted, respected, was warmed to with sense of kindness.

"Why could she not be like that to me? Why could she not believe in me?" Cyrilla asked sadly.

A very little turn, either way, with these two, now, would reveal to sweeter issues or shut up to more mistrust than ever. They had been too much alone together; now, possibly, they were a little in danger of some withdrawal through a larger friendly intercourse beyond themselves, and a too far-off and objective perception of each other. "If this is real, she has not been real with me," was the thought of each.

At least, however, they had been lifted into a fresher, safer atmosphere. They were not getting the reflected judgments of a lower social stratum. The "they says" or "they will says" of the Sharkes and Porbeagles were not whispering to their hearing or their apprehension.

If they could have lived on so a little longer, — if that had not happened which did happen, — but again — if? When it came, who shall say that it, also, was not sent of loving purpose for the two hearts and lives? Nothing less, it may be, would have so shown the whole truth between them; so stirred and impelled that which needed to break through the old barriers, change the old currents, and send a swift, strong force along the further lines of their waiting lives.

CHAPTER XVI.

KARMA.

" Was my father a bad man ? "

Rill asked this startling question of Miss Haven one day, suddenly. They were sitting together by the fire downstairs, while Miss Bonable took her forenoon nap above.

" My dear! why should you think I could know? And why do you ask ? " answered Miss Haven, with astonished accent.

" Because I think aunt Amelia has told you a great many things that she never would tell me ; and because — although I would not ask you to tell me more than you feel right — I think I have a right to know something ; and because," she went on very staidly and collectedly, " aunt Amelia has said so many times to me in the old worrying days, ' what 's bred in the bone will come out in the flesh.' It was horrid to hear her say that, Miss Haven ; it made me tremble all over with fear and anger, both ; it put me down ; it *dared* me to say another word. I never did dare ; it was always the end. She does n't say so now; she seems different. But she looks at me as if everything at all nice I try to do were a surprise; as if she could n't account for it; as if she wondered how *that*, by any accident, were bred in me."

Rill's voice, for all its controlled quietness, just broke a little. A troubled laugh, that was more pathetic than a sob, made way with the last words. Then she sat silent. It was a silence that demanded answer.

"No, Rill; your father never was a bad man. He was not, I suppose, in some essential things, a quite wise one. And because he was not wise in those special things, he was not just. It was not money, Rill," for Rill's eyes widened, and her lips parted with a mute inquiry. "It was something that came nearer. Your aunt Amelia cared for him, Cyrilla; and he *ought* to have belonged to her."

"And so," said Rill, slowly, after the pause in in which she took this strange thing in, " she never has believed in me." She thought she had the whole explanation now.

Miss Haven's hands lay on her lap with her work in them. She was looking over into Rill's face, with a hesitation in her own which the girl did not perceive. Presently she took up her knitting-needles again, and set two or three stitches. "I think we had better leave the matter there," she said.

Cyrilla's spirits rose almost lightly with a bound of relief. She had dreaded, she knew not what; this was so commonplace, so simple; so easy of excuse, perhaps. It was very queer to think of aunt Amelia so. "Was she ever pretty?" she asked. She almost asked if she had been ever young.

"I think she is pretty now; behind the hiding," said Miss Haven, quaintly.

Cyrilla laughed. "And loving too," she said, "behind the hardening?" The question came to her with instant hope. She put it gladly.

"Yes, you are right, Cyrilla. Sometimes a heart that can love most can harden most."

"And be most — suspecting?" This was asked reluctantly, but as if it need be asked. "Do you suppose she was that — may be — with my father?"

It had not escaped Miss Haven that such fact might have been. Her "I do not know," was negative admission.

"It is her way," said Cyrilla. "How she thinks of everything, I can't guess: but if you *were* up to the worst mischief, she would be beforehand. Her hands are held out in the dark ready for things to run against, even when they're not there. It makes you feel as if she must invent out of — consciousness. But I know she is a good woman.

Chiselwood gave her a word once that fitted; I've quoted it to her since, and made her very angry, when she has been pre-accusing me. It was very impertinent; because it was so — pertinent!"

" Chiselwood — impertinent!"

" Oh, no; he was complimentary, I suppose; it was my application that was pert. How many parts and turns there are to that word, Miss Haven! Chiselwood was putting in the new pantry window. She was afraid of its giving a chance to burglars; and she had a top bolt and a bottom bolt, and a wooden shutter, and an inside blind. ' They could slip *that* with a knife,' she said; or, ' they could cut *that* right out with a centre-bit and saw; they could feel where it was through the crack,' she kept suggesting. At last Chiselwood laid down his screwdriver and looked up at her: ' I think *you'd* make a pretty good burglar, mum,' he said. And then she hushed up, and walked off."

Miss Haven could but laugh.

" I'm afraid it's treacherous, my telling even you," said Rill. " I really *do* want to be true and kind; but why was I, just *I*, with just my faults, put precisely where I am, and in contact with — just such others? The world is made so queer, Miss Haven; and we are born so queerly!"

" I suppose we are born where we belong," said Miss Haven simply.

Rill heard her with a start. " Have *you* thought that ? " she cried.

" Thought what, my dear ? "

" That we have been before ? That we come into the places we have deserved ? That it is all our own ' natural selection ' ? " said Rill, with rapid impulse. The utterance was out of some keen, repressed thinking.

Miss Haven laid her hand over on both of Rill's, that were tightly clasped across her knee. " I have thought that ; and read it. It explains a great deal. It is the old Buddhist doctrine of Karma. But it needs a gospel to reach further. It is true, at any rate, from stage to stage of this life ; we come into what our choices and acts lead us to. If it should be true from life to life, if it has already brought us to our birth and place in this world, what then ? It is only more of it : a longer illustration. The fact and law remain ; and the necessity that we accept our *self* as our piece of human work and responsibility. We have each our own bit of evil to destroy, our own bit of the kingdom to build. We can be brave with that thought, can't we, Rill ? We can be thankful ; for we can redeem and vindicate not only our own lives, but lives that were before. We can prove the latent nobility of fatherhood and motherhood. It is the ' honoring ' of the fifth commandment.

Christianity takes us up where Buddhism drops us. My child!"—Miss Haven said, with eager tenderness, warming with her instant word that she felt was also a word for the time to come—"my dear child! Christ took upon himself our whole fallen humanity so: to redeem and restore it, even to itself; and to show that its real father-hood was in God!" Her face glowed, and tears stood in her eyes.

Rill's were large and tender too; a soft color came, and her lips took a gentler, quieter curve. But she said, still with a question, "Ah, dear Miss Haven, it is those 'acts and choices'! They are terrible; they come every minute, and we make so many mistakes; and then—we are in places where we were not meant to be!"

"Yes, the choice is now—every minute; 'now is the accepted time; now is the day of salvation.' It changes and shapes for us continually. But there is more than that; there is a choice beyond our own natural selection; something is chosen in us and for us, with help and hindrance. We are pre-vented. God is on our side. It is his own side."

"He puts us—he lets us be put, or put our-selves—in very hard places!"

Rill spoke slowly, half reluctantly, but still as if she must. She would not say so any more, but she could not yet understand why she and aunt Amelia should have been set to hinder each other; why, at least, they could not have been made to find each other out sooner and better. That which had been given her of late made it the stranger, somehow, that such had not been given before, or always.

" I will tell you something beautiful," said Miss Haven, " that fits just there. It only came to me the other day — in time for you. I have a new treasure — an ' emphasized New Testament,' in which the readings give the old Greek idioms and order of importance in the wordings. And I found this: ' *I*,' — the ' I ' was a heavy capital, — ' as many soever as I may be tenderly loving, am convicting, and putting under discipline : be zealous, therefore, and repent.' We cannot conquer ourselves until we are convicted of ourselves ; we cannot ' grow warm,' ' be zealous,' and ' turn back,' until this tenderly - loving discipline compels — urges *with* us ! ' "

Rill's head took a lower bend ; the soft eyes veiled themselves ; she could not say another word.

She carried that about with her for days.

" *I*, as many as I may be tenderly loving, am convicting, and putting under discipline."

Her whole life looked comforted to her ; it was as if she saw it lying in God's hand. A hope kept

breathing up into her spirit. Not a hope, so defined, for the future; it was a hope for the past;
that it had not been all wrong, — all punishment.
She had been convicted, that she might conquer.
She had been let run on into fault — into darkness
— that she might desire to turn and come back
into the truth, the light. A noble ardor was born
in her; she knew what that old word meant, —
" be zealous." She said in her heart, " I will
choose and act, not for myself, but for the right.
Myself will be taken care of."

CHAPTER XVII.

"YOU MAY, MY CHILD."

UPON this mood there came an unlooked-for happening; a gladness that surprised, and searched her also; a two-edged word of God.

Putnam King was not a helpless person; he only yielded to circumstances until he could fashion other circumstances to counteract them.

One day, a little while before the early dinner at the cottage, which was prompt at this time to the noonstreak on the kitchen floor, — when Clementhy was making up some special savoriness for the meal, after which would come Miss Bonable's twenty-minute nap, and then her game of backgammon with Mrs. Rospey, who had promised her the afternoon, — a carriage rolled smoothly to the little front gate. A pair of noble horses, whose spirit and training showed in beautiful equilibrium with every movement, brought it swiftly to its stopping-place, and drew up there as cleanly and promptly as they had sped along. Putnam King was on the forward seat, and held the reins.

Cyrilla came down toward the open door, over the straight little staircase that nearly reached the threshold.

"Has my aunt come round here yet, Miss Raye?" asked the young man, across the shoulder of Miss Pond, who had emerged below and appeared at the entrance; but who, finding her service superfluous, and not wont to hold herself in any needless waiting, walked unperturbed away.

"No," Cyrilla answered, "Miss Haven has not been here to-day."

"I thought she would be here; I will drive over to the Corner for her; she will be ready. Miss Cyrilla, will you put on your wraps meanwhile? She wishes you to go round Grayfells with her. It is a lovely day. Don't mind dinner; we must take the heart of the sunshine; we are to have a carriage lunch."

Rill hesitated; she was taken unprepared; she could not quite understand. Miss Haven had said nothing of this plan. But to-day was such a beautiful surprise of autumn weather; it could not have been counted on. We may say that it had been counted on, and very eagerly watched for by Mr. Putnam King. Such days do come, though they give no notice, even away on into November; they are the golden-ripe days of the year. Now that it had arrived, he had ordered his line of action in such a way as to preclude defeat.

Rill was lost for a moment looking at the well equipped carriage and the driver who so gracefully held the reins. " I wonder," she thought, " if I must n't. I wonder if I may."

" Thank you. I do not know." Rill said, after but a few moments' perceptible hesitation. " I will see. When Miss Haven comes — I could be ready in a moment, if I were to go. It would be *very* pleasant," she added, as fearing she had taken such a kindness with too scant recognition.

" It *will* be very pleasant," said Putnam King, with a bright smile, and the light lift of the reins which gave the signal to his horses. He turned them neatly between wall and wall, over the turf sides, coming close to the gateway as he brought them round, and leaning with a backward glance toward her before he let them take their pace. " We shall be here again directly," were his last words; and the carriage passed beyond the ash-tree, over the soft bed of leaves, old-gold and bronze, that lay heaped and strewn far out around its foot.

" I wonder," Rill repeated slowly, " if I must n't. I wonder — if I may."

" It is only one — pleasant — afternoon," she still deliberated, going up the stairs. " It is with Miss Haven — why should I refuse her? I must learn not to want more than I can get; but what comes to me, why should n't I take? I will leave it to aunt Amelia," she concluded rapidly. "If she makes the slightest objection, if she wants me for the least thing, that shall settle it. I *do* want to be shown; I *don't* want to do all the choosing by myself."

It was not a blind fate she was invoking; in her heart there was a prayer. Without looking for the thing that made her fearful, without such allowing as would force directly a struggle that would shame her, she began to find her choices perilous, to realize in a dim way how she needed to be given a "right judgment in all things," and to be "kept continually" in a "holy comfort." She wanted that mothering in the spirit, of which the child, in its first mothering, learns the beautiful sign.

"Aunt Amelia," she said, entering the pleasant south chamber where Miss Bonable, in her big, white easy-chair, sat by the garden window, "Mr. Putnam King has just been here, with a carriage and a message from Miss Haven. They want me to be ready for a drive with them, round Grayfells. It will take all the afternoon. Could you spare me, or had I better not go?"

The odor of Clementhy's chicken stew was stealing up to Miss Amelia's nostrils; her knitting-work was all arranged in the wide red basket at her side; the backgammon table was out and

open ; all the momentary surroundings were sub-
tilely propitious.   But it was not altogether these ;
she was pleased with Cyrilla's straightforward
manner ; she was grateful to her ; she had some
half-fledged hope of her ; her real love for the girl
pleaded for indulgence.

" I sha'n't want you," she replied. " Martha
Rospey is coming, and will stay to tea. Clementhy 's got corn-muffins and sweet apples and cream.
I 'm going to knit on my quilt ; I sha'n't play *all*
the time."

Aunt Amelia had a rigorous conscience, even
over her own invalid amusements. She was honest, also, clear through.   " Martha Rospey is going
to bring her board, and show me Polish backgammon," she added ; "though I don't much expect I
shall like it."

Cyrilla took her leading with a light heart. It
was as if somebody, beyond, though by word of
aunt Amelia, had said to her lovingly, " You may,
my child."

She was ready at the door when the carriage
was driven back. Nobody could have guessed
from Miss Haven's manner that she had been
routed by her nephew from a peaceful nap, to be
told that she wanted to go round Grayfells with
Miss Raye and himself, and that Miss Raye was
waiting for them at the cottage. " You are not to

mind dinner," he said, as he had said to Cyrilla.
" I've got a whole basketful of deliciousness put
up at your Woman's Exchange."

" But look at all this," Miss Haven had said,
sitting up against her sofa pillow. " I was going
to be so busy, presently." " All this " was a confusion of ribbon-and-lace boxes and piece-baskets,
with an array of half a dozen charming little
bisque-faced dolls leaning in semicircle around the
deep cushion of an armchair. " I was to finish
some of these to-day ; the fair begins next Monday. How can I leave them ? "

" How can you leave Miss Raye and me ? *These*
girls don't want matronizing," said Putnam King.

" You naughty, double-dealing boy ! " aunt Elizabeth had exclaimed. And then she had got up
and sent him off while she put on her other gown
and her bonnet.

" I am so glad you are going with us," she said
with veracious inconsistence to Rill Raye when she
found her at the doorstep.

Her guile was like her gossip ; the one became
truth, as the other became benediction, in its utterance.

CHAPTER XVIII.

THE broad back seat of the low carriage curved forward at the ends; the corners were perfect for lounging, and it was easy for the occupant of the driving-seat, by a half turn, to face either of those behind. Rill took the left-hand place; it was upon the side nearest as they had drawn up. Putnam King naturally kept to the right. He managed the lines easily, and as easily gave half his attention at the backward diagonal.

It was the very last day of October; one of those days that only come in the afterglow of the year; different from summer weather, different from the gorgeousness of early autumn; but tender, inexpressibly, with a warmth that was like love loath to leave, — still, peaceful, waiting; a kindliness of Heaven and a trustingness of earth.

The trees — all but here and there a few — had given up their fleeting beauty of summer leafage and of dazzling color; they stood in their grace and strength of gloriously arching boughs crowning their pillared majesty, their veiling lacework of interweaving stems outlining exquisitely against the blue that pressed itself into their myriad-formed interstices in wonderful mosaic. The smells of fruitage lingered in the air ; odors of cedar, pine and fern came drifting from the woods ; as they entered the forest road behind the town, they came into the full deliciousness of these, upon which the sun lay fervent.

The way lay first along that North Road, beyond Brook Lane, running between the pines and chestnuts of the Crooke domain and the wide-stretching woodland on the other hand, rich in oak and beech, and rising into high pasture-downs, upon which stood clumps and spires of evergreens against the sky.

This rise of land was the beginning of the Gray-fells ; a few miles up there was a break between the heightening cliffs where the road wound in and through ; then it went up along the northeastwardly trend again, with the fells upon the right. Far over in the outskirts of Wewachet, in the sparsely-built farm region, there was a turn over the ridge itself, where, with a long ascending slope, the crest was reached and passed. And down upon the east incline you came into woods and pastures and farm-fields again. through whose alternating pleasant-ness was gained once more, after the wide circuit, the entrance into Old Village ; and so, for our friends, the coming back from Tide Point home. This was the drive " around Grayfells."

" This north way round is the prettiest bit of drive, I think, in all the country here," said Mr. King, as they rolled noiselessly along the soft, brown, natural road, untouched by the offense of McAdam, and entered under the warm, spicy shade of the pine woods.

" The way we seldom have a chance to go is apt to seem the prettiest. This is outside our beaten tracks ; we only come for pleasure. If we usually had to take this road, we should think the sunshiny stretch along the meadows delightful, I suppose." There was a happy little thrill in Cyrilla's voice as she spoke, Miss Haven leaving the reply to her.

" Yes ; there 's a charm in the unusual. And in the sense of special possession, too. We have this all to ourselves, for the time being, as if nobody else ever came this way. A common thoroughfare is a dull thing. What everybody does, or has, every day, we do not care for. We like to find our own pathways, or to think we do ; even if they are only what all the generations before have trodden out for us. Life is a queer thing."

" It is lived queerly," Rill rejoined, involuntarily. And then, as if she had taken more to herself than she had meant to, and was getting further into analytics than was quite fitting for her with Putnam King, while his aunt, to whom he belonged, sat by, she shifted both talk and address with a pretty *insouciance.*

" Did you know, Miss Haven, that the green ridge over there has always been called Rattlesnake Hill ? What an ugly name, is n't it, to be fastened to a beautiful spot ? "

" Yes ; but if the ugly things were fastened there, it was safe, perhaps, to give it a true calling," said Miss Haven.

" I 'm afraid there would be plenty of ugly names," said Putnam King, " if we had fair warning of everything in the christening. It is only now and then that a thing, or a person, gets named after the fact."

" But then, you see," said Rill, " the fact may change, and the name stays. *That* is n't fair. I don't think there has been a rattlesnake on that hill for years."

" Did they all come down into Wewachet ? "

Rill laughed. " May be they did, " she said. " There have been a good many killed, I 've been told. I never saw one."

" Perhaps that 's your innocence. You had better look out for the rattle. I think I 've heard it. People may be bitten, sometimes, before they know of the danger."

" If you like to talk parables, why can't you find pleasant ones ? " put in Miss Haven, who had yet not been able herself to keep from laughing a little, with Rill. " There must be plenty, I think, among all these beautiful things."

" It is well, however, to have done first with the rattlesnakes," said the young man, with satisfaction.

Somehow, Cyrilla felt a trouble put away from her — a sting removed, or fended off — in this light nonsense of Mr. King's. Under it he had managed that she should catch some fine inference that no venom had been able to poison his thought of her ; no impertinence of tongues had meddled with her to her harm with him. Not that she made the least bit more of the inference than that; it was only that he would not have so spoken had any foolishness she had been afraid of had weight with him against her.

She felt freed to be happy ; simply happy again in the friendliness that she would be so sorry to lose. She ceased to catechise herself, even in that smothered self-questioning which hurts the more that it covers itself, ashamed or dreading to be ashamed, from direct and open thought. Her one pleasant afternoon had begun with a strange and sudden burst of blessed sunshine. She was so buoyantly content that she could not immediately trouble her content again with words. She sat silent, while now and then Miss Haven and her nephew talked casually, with brief remarks that did not grow to conversation.

Out beyond the woods they came to a certain broad swell that seemed to raise itself as a centre, zenithward, whence the horizon line, broken and closed in here and there by scattered forest growth, fell away from the slight, beautiful uplift, leaving it in nearer communion with the sky.

"Stop here a minute, Put," said Miss Haven, reaching out her hand. Mr. King reined in, gently; they came instantly to a stand.

"There!" said Miss Haven. "Now look up. Did you ever see the blue and the clouds so near? And yet we are not very high. I have noticed it here, and in one other place, — in cousin Sarah's brook-orchard. I have walked there at twilight, when there seemed a close tent of the loveliest colors dropping just overhead and about me. I have seemed to be right *in* the sunset."

"Here we are in the blue shine and the soft whiteness. It is wonderful. What makes it?"

"We are a little shut in as to our horizon, and we are just a little lifted above it," said Putnam King.

"Yes, that is it!" said Miss Haven, with a joyful accent. "You have explained the correspondence. That makes it lovelier than ever."

"I did n't intend any Swedenborgianism," said Putnam, laughing.

"No. It was there. That is what I am glad of."

"We shall come to something wider by and by. You will be glad of that, too, won't you, Miss Raye?"

"I think I am glad of everything, in a day like this," said Rill.

"Little horizons and all?"

"Yes. A horizon is always rolling away. There is no real line and end. That is something to make one very happy." The ring in her voice was like clear-rippling water-music.

"I like to see you thoroughly happy, Miss Rill," said Putnam King.

CHAPTER XIX.

THE HAPPY HOUSETOP.

THEN they drove on again. From this point the old road diverted gradually from its skirting of Grayfells. It was the original thoroughfare around by North Shepaug, across the further shoulder of Rattlesnake Hill. The new way, over the fells, branched before the curve had widened far, and crossed diagonally the level space upon the right, to the first reach of the eastward ascent. The two tracks formed a broad-forked, slant-stemmed Y.

Through a cut in the Rattlesnake ridge was being run a piece of railway; a bit of cross section, uniting two main lines. In its progress it had come through upon the old road, just beyond the fork; they were laying the track, now, at grade. Beyond, it was to follow its course, northeastwardly, under the diminishing slopes of Grayfells.

Putnam King had not thought of this work at all; of course he could not have known that it would have reached this precise point to-day. Just before they came to their own safe turn, therefore, they faced suddenly the hindrance and confusion. There was something startling to equine nerve in the abrupt surprise of the swarming groups, the bright red shirts, the obstruction.

" Go on, boys ! "

It was but a cheery little word, uttered almost quietly, with a careless rising inflection. The steady hand at the same instant made itself just felt along the communicating lines. It was the connecting of the human nerve — cool, adequate, assured — with the possible flutter of the animal. It was enough, and it was beforehand. The beautiful beasts lifted their heads and curved their backs with the perception and the check that might have been a fright, but was changed to a confidence ; and obeyed the guidance which turned them aside upon the crisp, green level. The way lay safely enough along this wide, turfy margin, even quite past the cumber of rails and sleepers, and the bristle and motion of crowbars, picks and men. The direction they were now to take would lead them comfortably off from all.

They were just striking their side road from this short cut over the grass, and entering the fringing thicket of birches at the fell-foot, when the sound of a shout and a rush arrested them. A glance backward showed them an impending disaster.

Some other steed had been less sagaciously manageable, or less adroitly managed. A frightened

horse, attached to a low, broad, heavy buggy, had
wheeled to the left and bolted, but been brought up
at the roadside, upon which it had come round in
its wild turn, among granite blocks strewn and
heaped upon the grass in process of the railway
construction. There the vehicle had been caught;
it stood with one wheel raised, leaning at a frightful angle, and held fast; the horse leaped and
reared frantically among the stones, coming down
each time against the rough corners and edges
which wounded and infuriated him, and at every
upward spring threatening to fall backward upon
the carriage and its occupants.

"Those men are fools! They are only frighten-
ing the creature more!" said Putnam King, half
rising from his seat with the impulse to go and
help. The laborers, in their blazing attire, and
with their shouts and crowding, had gathered im-
potently around the struggling animal, unable as
yet to get foothold where they could cope with him,
or even to make close approach.

"Go, Mr. King. I can hold the reins," said
Rill.

She was out, as she spoke, by the low step
between the guards, and up with a spring to the
footboard of the forward seat. Putnam King
glanced quickly in her face, met the large, steady
eyes, and put the lines in her hands without a word.

The next instant he had come round by the heads of the horses, given them a quiet, caressing pat and stroke, said in that same cheery tone of friendly 'rapport, "You know better, boys, don't you?" and was off with the same breath over the intervening bit of sward and roadway to the rescue.

The wildly excited horse had twice sprung from the grasp of the men who had tried to seize and hold him by the head; had actually carried one of them dangling up into the air to lose his hold as he came down, and roll back among the blocks of granite, scratched and terrified.

Putnam King sprang up on one of the stones just forward of the reach of the dangerous fore-feet, and held his arms outspread. "So! So!" he cried; not plunging or grasping at the animal, but facing him, with strong word and gesture of command and reassurance. "*So! quiet!* Who-a! good horse!"

The extended arms, the determined, friendly eye, the tone of sympathetic control, of good faith and mastery, prevailed presently over even brute panic; the creature paused between his springs as if for possible help. Two resolute hands met a well-watched chance, and came each side upon the bridle. "So!—So!" and the horse stayed down. Then one hand loosed its hold, and stroked and soothed him. "Good horse!" the kind, strong voice repeated. The danger was over.

Some of the red-shirted men had helped the people from the buggy; they were an elderly man and his wife. The latter had been upon the downward side; they lifted her over the wheels and stones; then her husband made his way, and stood beside her. Plenty of hands detached the broken thills and harness; the horse was led forth, free and trembling.

Mr. King took one of the cushions and carried it to a comfortable place. "You had better sit down and rest, madam," he said, offering her his arm.

The old gentleman was pale and dazed. He looked ruefully at the disordered, dislocated group, — his wife with torn gown and twisted bonnet, his horse with cut knees, his wrecked conveyance.

"Just wait," Putnam told them, "I will be back again presently; we will see what can be done. Where were you going?"

"To North Shepaug; we live there," was the answer from the man.

"We're the — minister; I mean he is," his wife said, and laughed tremulously at her own bewildered announcement.

Putnam King was back beside his own carriage.

"It is the minister and his wife from North Shepaug. They are like the babes in the wood, or Adam and Eve just let out into the wilderness. I think I ought to go and take them home."

"Of course you ought, Putnam," said aunt Elizabeth, with alacrity, stepping off the carriage with the word. "Rill and I can wait here quite comfortably."

"You poor old lady! I quite forgot how uncomfortable you might be with only feminine hands upon the reins. You are sure you won't be afraid now?"

"Not in the least. What should there be to be afraid of?"

"There is a nice little place up there at the right, just off the road. I meant we should take our lunch there. You and Miss Raye can begin."

"We won't touch a crumb!"

"We won't even peep to see what crumbs there are!" The two women spoke in fugue, indignantly.

"I shall be gone less than twenty minutes, very likely," said Mr. King.

They found the place he told them of, a little hillside space, hedged in with hemlocks spicy in the sun; the rocky shelf which made its floor carpeted with crisp, short turf and pale-green, glistening moss; these spotted and flecked with gold by the fallen leaves of the delicate small birches.

"What a lovely little corner!" said Miss Haven, as they sat down and looked and smelled about with delight.

"What a lovely, wonderful corner *to-day* is!" said Rill Raye.

"'All the corners' — of the earth and life — are in His hands," said aunt Elizabeth, simply. And then, with readiest turn to the commonest pleasant things of the instant, "I wonder what Put *has* got in that big basket!" I half think she meant a further, higher suggestion. At any rate, I know Rill Raye thought of the giving of the bread and the great baskets full that might be waiting.

Within the twenty minutes, back came Put. "They live just in the northeast corner," he said. "Indeed, the minister told me that the kitchen and woodshed are over the line, in Wewachet. The man who lives with him, and runs the farm on shares, sleeps over the woodshed, and votes in Wewachet; but the minister sleeps and pays taxes and preaches and goes to town-meeting in Shepaug. He does n't seem to think it matters about a house divided against itself."

He chattered on as he brought out the basket, and opened it. He could have chattered about anything. Apparently enough, it was a lovely corner in time to him also.

Without a direct word to herself, it made Rill glad to see him so. Perhaps she wondered, just a little, that he did not make allusion to her bold holding of his horses. She did not want praise;

she did not magnify her service, to her own thought; but she would have liked if he had thought it something. Nevertheless, she was as glad, almost, as she could be.

For Putnam King, he was not so foolish as to waste his advantage even in a word. What he thought about it could be turned to better account than in a passing thanks or even honoring comment, which would have dismissed the matter with a half using of its capabilities in point. He had in him finer qualifications for the bar than that.

There was a good deal to comment upon with satisfaction in what he called the " woman's grub." " Positively," he said, " they show their sense in this part of their business."

Delicate buttered rolls, delicious little chicken pâtés; thin, pink shavings of ham, curled up like rose-leaves; coffee, richly creamed, in a bottle; crisp wafers, only known to the W. E., that crackle delightfully in the mouth, and then melt; great grapes that crowded each other on their stems, with cheeks purple-black in winy fullness; even a tiny lunch-bouquet for each person, on a napkin; these, the lifted lid and carefully exploring fingers brought to light, and appetites, touched to keen appreciation by the elixir of October air, did thoroughly enjoy.

When, a little later, they came out upon the

broad, bare, breeze-and-sun-swept top of Grayfells, the rest and sweetness joined themselves to a great, free revelation. The horses stopped, as if it were of their own accord; their accord was with their driver; they threw up their fine heads as if they recognized with their own joy the height, the expanse; they stood still, not just because it was welcome after the steep climb, but with some pause of unmistakable pleasure in what the climb had gained; their eyes gleamed, their nostrils were dilated; the splendid light, the pure, keen air, seemed to fill them with all their nature could take in of breath and brilliance; at what precise point their nature stopped, replete, who shall undertake to say?

Putnam King stood by them; the others were out of the carriage, also, upon the level, rocky summit, where wheel-tracks vanished and feet trod buoyantly.

"Ah, *this* is the happy housetop!" Putnam King exclaimed, flinging out his arms with jubilant freedom. "This is the wide place I told you of! We are rid of circumstance up here; we are let loose; there is nothing but circumambience!"

"What a boy you are!" his aunt said, smiling.

"Yes; and you are a girl; that is just what is let loose in us when we get out of things like this. Is n't it good, Miss Raye?"

"I never was up here, before," Rill answered slowly. Her delight was grave; its tone was quieted with its own amazement.

"I am glad of that," the young man said, as he drew nearer to her. Away down, on either hand, they had left it all; they looked back upon it as they had never seen it seem before. Sunshine and gentle shadows were upon everything; the villages, the mills by the river, the spires, the bosks of woods, the threads of highway, thin and wandering; the shining reach of the Wewachet, the winding loops of the Shepaug; the broad, united tidal stream, the little bay; in the far southeastern distance, the silver glitter defining the sea-line.

Putnam pointed this out to his companions. "That makes it perfect," he said. " Why do you suppose it does? Why is there nothing like the sea to *satisfy* a landscape? "

" It is the encompassing life," Miss Haven answered. "It is that which feeds the earth, and lies all around it, without end. 'The power of an endless life,' " she repeated softly, to herself.

" Then why is there to be 'no more sea'? "

"Just for the reason that there is to be no more sun. It will be Light and Life direct, and typeless. The Lord himself will be sea and sun."

Something of the rapture of that was in the time and place. It was the inspiration of the heights. They were silent under it. But without speech, in such surroundings, the hearts of human beings are held near.

They were not sure how long they had been there when Miss Haven said: "The sun is getting low behind us; we had better, I think, go down."

Once more in the carriage the descent did not take long. The road followed at first a natural terracing, turning this way and that, from slope to slope that merged one into another; then it fell rapidly through a dark forest piece, to the level; they came out upon the common way again, that carried them toward the Point; just this side of Old Village, by a cross-road and a turn, they bore round homeward.

They were presently at Crooke Corner; the sun was far down, westward; the heights and their day were behind them.

"I will leave you first, aunt Elizabeth; your dolly-babies need you."

"Oh, thanks!" said aunt Elizabeth, with an accent.

When they came to the door, however, Rill Raye alighted, also. "I am to take two dollies home to dress, you know," she said. "Good-by, Mr. King; it has been beautiful. I shall remember it all winter."

CHAPTER XX.

PUTNAM KING did not say good-by. "I shall be back before you go home," he answered her. The words conveyed a telephonic meaning to Miss Haven; they gave plainly an injunction,— "keep her."

The good lady did not quite know about that; she discerned purpose in Cyrilla, also. What she did not allow for, after all, was the deeper foresight and strategy of Putnam King.

He knew very well that Rill Raye would scarcely let herself be driven home by him alone from Crooke Corner, in that unnecessarily obvious way; he did not suppose she would stay long at Miss Haven's, either; she would walk off almost directly; he would rather she would be just conscious enough to do that. She would almost certainly take the pleasant cross-cut to the North Road, through the chestnut wood. It was precisely the walk he wished to take with her.

A few rods down the street he met the extra man

from Oates's, coming with the depot driver from the
3.50 train; this, again, being a wisely preordained
circumstance. To him he resigned his own team,
and retraced his way rapidly on foot.

He was just in time to catch the glimpse he had
expected, of Cyrilla crossing the orchard edge to
the wood-lot. In the opening of the glade path
between the great trees, he overtook her. "I told
you I would be back," he said. "And this is just
the way I meant to take you home. The day
would not have been quite perfect without this.
One does not care to go by beaten, dusty tracks,
after the real highways."

It was what Cyrilla had felt; it was the instinct
of her own choice, and he had divined it of her.
They passed on under the great arching boughs
into the sweet dimness of the nutwood.

"You held those horses bravely, to-day."

Cyrilla turned her face toward him in surprise.
She had thought that matter passed over, as a trifle
done with. Now he spoke of it, it looked a trifle,
though she had been a little glad and proud of it,
before.

"Why, it was not brave, at all," she said. "They
held themselves; I knew they would. You trusted
them; they understood that you put them on their
honor to be good with me." As she spoke, she
understood herself; it had been just that she had
been proud of.

" The courage was in your comprehending; courage is only confidence in the right working of things. Misgiving is what makes afraid. To believe is to be brave."

They were words from him which made her heart beat. Strong, fine words, out of a right, high thinking. She was glad of it in him; she was glad that he would speak it so to her.

" They were such lovely horses," she said. She could only put her thrill of feeling into words of them.

" Yes; they are the sort a man can establish a relation with. Horses, in harness, are but an extension of human nerves and temperament. There must be sympathy; then you can do anything. Only, the human must keep just ahead of the brute; it must feel and anticipate, this is all. You must expect the unexpected, and keep in touch upon the lines. Then you won't be run away with."

" Ah, that is true in more than driving horses ! "

" Yes: in driving one's self. Self-control is a grand thing; it gives a man a share in the government of the universe." The young man's head was lifted, as he spoke. He was conscious of his own harness in the divine order of things.

" But one does n't always have the reins in one's own hands," said Rill.

" Not ? Not the very self-holding reins ? "

" Well, yes ; behind everything, and, after all, I suppose one has. But one is driven, too ; and the driving is n't always sympathetic."

" I think aunt Elizabeth would insist that it was. I think she would quote something about being ' touched with a feeling of our infirmities.' I suppose she would say that all driving not left to us is really in such hands, Miss Raye."

Rill was silent ; he could not know what made her so ; that it was the very stir in her that made her still.

" I understood you, though," he said. " I could n't have spoken for myself, so I had to quote aunt Elizabeth. I have been restive enough with some driving ; and just to see the sort of compulsion others have been under has infected me with a rebellion. Yet, after all, the good words are true, and worth reminding of. I would like to give you the best, Miss Rill."

" But I have not made you understand me," Rill broke forth. " I have been unfair. I was thinking of things that are all past. I have no right to speak so now, only — if it could have seemed so sooner — I should have driven myself better. That is the real trouble." She spoke the last words more quietly. and with a smile.

" Don't go back, Miss Rill, for any trouble ; we

are in to-day," he answered her. When he said
"Miss Rill," there was a singular, gentle drawing
near, with a restraint of waiting, in the accent;
it seemed to tell her more than she dared believe.
His word " to-day " had a ring of triumph in it.

"Oh, to-day has been a beautiful day!" she
said. He had led her back into the joy of it.

" Yes ; I hope we shall have more to-days. But
a man must not look for beautiful days that he has
not earned. To-morrow, Miss Rill, I begin my
earning. Will you wish me well in it?"

" I wish you well in everything, Mr. King."

" Some time I may come back and remind you
of your saying that." He paused slightly, and
then went on. " I shall be away; I shall not see
you so often; I shall be proving myself. It is
what I must do, first of all. I did not mean
money, when I spoke of earning; I have enough
of that to make it needful to assert myself in other
things. Aunt Elizabeth is right; I must begin a
man's life before I can ask of life what a man
wants. You have only seen me as a boy, Miss
Raye." He withdrew into the distance of the
formal name. Truly, he had great self-control —
the thing he had declared was grand — this boy!

" I have not seen you as a boy to-day. You
have been doing things — and saying things —
that I shall remember — shall thank you for,

always," Rill Raye answered him softly, yet keeping safely and carefully to the patent and acknowledged. Silence would not have been so safe; it would have seemed expectant.

She did not know what it was she was afraid, or tremulously happy, to expect; she knew it was not coming now, at once, and she acted from the instinct, on her own part, to help turn it by. But how different all this was from that other woodwalk, that other "explanation;" what a nobler putting off! The one put *her* off — from an inference he was not ready yet to verify; the other — this other — put himself off from some hope he had not earned.

"I do not mean to give up boyishness; I hope nobody will give me up because of it. The manliest man I know — my father — is a boy at heart, and openly at times, as much as I am."

Rill did not say of what that reminded her instantly, — the little child in the midst, who was the greatest.

"One does not care to show one's deepest, always," he went on. "There are things not to be spoken of to everybody; and only sometimes to anybody."

They were the things he had spoken of to her. She had no answer now.

"I do not think we need to be always saying

them to ourselves; we should wear them out with
repetitions: we just know they are there; that is
enough to build up life on, and life will show.
You wish me well, then, in my building?"

They had come through into the clearer light.
They were at the end of the dim aisle of trees. He
stopped, and turned toward her, looking into her
face. He held out his hand. She put hers in it.
"I wish you well," she said, again, in her clear
voice, meeting his look with beautiful, true eyes.

"I *want* you to wish me well. I want you to
believe in me — as I believe in you," he said.

They were near the cottage now; the forest path
came out close to Brook Lane. He crossed with
her, and saw her to her door; he stood upon the
threshold, and Miss Bonable came forth and met
them. He had a frank, courteous word for her;
then he said a simple good-night to both, and went
away, notwithstanding that aunt Amelia invited
him to come in to tea.

"Another time, if you ask me," he said, with a
charming deference.

"That's a clever young man," remarked Miss
Bonable, following Rill in. "He comes to the door.
I like people that come to the door and don't stay
behind the fences. He speaks up, and he's got
behavior."

Rill ran up to her room; there was a window to

the east, and Brook Lane ran eastward. She saw Mr. King walking down between the trees. The twilight was yet golden about him; he was going to his work in the world. He had left her here, where her work was, but it was light here also.

She went down, without selfish lingering. Miss Bonable was waiting for her tea. She told to her and Mrs. Rospey the happy story of her day; all but the happy, hidden, intangible heart of it that it was not possible to utter. She ate muffins and sweet apple and cream; she helped Clementhy clear away afterward, and she washed carefully the delicate old spoons and the china cups and the pictured India plates; she put all by, and then she sat and read the evening paper to aunt Amelia. When she had done all this — it was scarcely more than an hour's work, but it had a blessed lifetime in it — she went with Miss Bonable to her bed-room, and arranged her for the night. After the tired head was upon the pillow that she placed pre-cisely for completest rest, she leaned down and kissed the lips that had been so often harsh with hard rebuke. "Good-night," she said. Good-night was in her heart for all the world.

"Good-night, Rill; you 've fixed me very nice; I 'm glad you 've had your treat."

That was much for aunt Amelia to have said, and she had called her "Rill." A stiff "Cy-rilla" or " Rill Raye," with objurgative emphasis upon the surname, were what the girl had been mostly used to from her; but aunt Amelia had grown different; everything had grown different now.

Rill went again into her own little east room, away into her own new world.

" As I believe in you."

That word set her free of her old, hard past; it put her on probation for a strange, vague, beautiful future. That it was vague, that nothing was clear and promised, she was glad; she would not have had it put before her as a certainty, for all the world. She had not " earned " it yet. She, too, must earn something. She must earn his faith. She must earn — whatever he might tell her by and by.

A great, calm moon came climbing up the sky. It poured its light round her, wrapping her in its white veil. She sat there in a wonderful, shining peace. It was the moon of Halloween.

CHAPTER XXI.

FINE WINTRY COLD.

DURING the weeks that followed, Miss Bonable rapidly resumed the vigor and the habits of her life. She was about the domicile everywhere, searching into its needs of housewifery that had accumulated from delay, and setting herself and Clementhy Pond and Cyrilla unmitigatingly to work; and Rill surprised her aunt with the genuine readiness of her participation and help.

It was not mere conscientious obedience to another's will ; it was putting her own will to it with a pleasure. All the secret Miss Bonable could not know : the rousing, with a woman's hope, of all the true practical woman's instinct. But she began to be glad in the child, with a tremulous joy, like that of one new-born in spiritual things. If it would only last !

I do not mean to say that it was Heaven all at once at Brook Lane cottage, any more than it is with the hopeful convert. The old peremptoriness of character would now and then assert itself.

Cyrilla could not, on her part, spring at once to
full-grown thrift and judgment ; there were lapses,
even of industry, and consequent little jars ; but
there was a new atmosphere in which the tendency
was not to storm, but to placid weather.

Abroad, something of a social life began again,
and with more freedom for Rill. When the second
invitation came to visit Mrs. Rextell, aunt Amelia
said : " You go, Rill ; it's more for you than
me, though they're polite, and I appreciate it. I
ain't up to evenings out, yet ; and I'm bright
enough to know I ain't quite up to the Rextells
any way. I'm only glad the real stuff is in them
to find out real stuff in other people. You go ;
it'll do you good."

Clementhy was scrupulously dispatched at the
close of these evenings to accompany Rill home.
Mrs. Rextell would have provided for that ; but
Miss Bonable was persistent. " If one friend sees
her home, another may ; it's best to understand,
as a rule, that it's to be Clementhy." Mrs. Rextell perceived and approved.

Rill was growing into one of those friendships
which lift a girl up, in certain peculiar feminine
ways, even more than the larger, separate feminine
experience. They bring into a higher womanly
form the things that may, as yet, have been crude
in her, though fair and noble. They help her to

realize that which she would fain be, before the asking comes to which she would give the best of her possible attaining. She trims her lamp in the sweet company of the other wise virgins, that when the bridegroom calls she may have it burning.

There was something reverential in Rill's regard for Margaret Rextell; the kind of worship which differs from external or circumstantial admiration, in that it is a spiritual discernment which perhaps only a woman, perhaps only a girl, and she for one of her own sex, can feel. It is angel-worship. I do not mean adoration; that is only for the Highest; but from rank to rank, through spiritual degrees, up to the archangels, the seven spirits round the throne, the joy of worth-ship goes up and up, lifting those who are capable, and through a divine fellowship ranging them to higher and higher plane and place, even beforehand. It is the golden stair; and they who reach down loving, holy hands are they who sit on the thrones, under their Lord, adjudging, in their order, the tribes of the blessed Israel.

Rill went also to Connie Norris's. She would not desert old friendship; if good came to her from farther up, why should she not share it, if she could, with one not yet quite high enough to hunger for it? What had made herself to hunger, save the bringing near to her of what should feed her best? She hardly thought of it so — she certainly did not assume a mission — but she came among them with a difference; she brought a new air, not of affectation, but a simple breath of life, a gracious contagion of wholesomeness.

Connie asked her, and made much of her, not for the gift of healing, but because she could so command other presence that she wanted. Dr. Harriman would come when Cyrilla could be met; Connie had found out that, and acknowledged it to herself. She had acuteness to perceive that her own old flirtation was over; but she did not want all the world to see it, and suddenly. She meant to keep up a light social intimacy, an apparent power that need not be too obviously defined, until she herself might seem deliberately to have made up her own mind and choice.

It was at Connie Norris's, one evening, that a little talk arose which Rill had after-reason to remember. I say, "Connie Norris's" without reference to the elders of the family, or any literal house ownership or authority, because for social purposes, and at Connie's time and pleasure, it was not Mr. and Mrs. Norris's house at all. According to the charming construction of things in certain spheres of modern life, the parents were, upon such occasions, nowhere; nowhere being, more strictly speaking, a little back hall-parlor devoted to newspapers, cigars, the mending-basket and the cribbage-board.

Connie and her set were planning some regular winter sociables for dancing and theatricals ; they were to be held at the village assembly rooms ; and were to be made the events, the counting-points, of the season for Wewachet. " You will join, of course," they said to Dr. Harriman.

" Of course I shall be happy to have the privilege," the doctor answered. " But practically, I cannot take part in them at first. I expect to be in Canada, with my sister, for a while."

" And leave us all wailing — and gnashing our teeth ! " said the irrepressible Connie, not very nice about a joke.

" I hope not. I hope you can spare me, both socially and professionally, for the few weeks I may be away."

" Where does Mrs. Stanesby live ? "

" In Ottawa."

" Oh, you will see everything ! Princess Louise — no, Lady Somebody, now, is n't it ? Who is the Governess-General ? You 'll be there for the carnival ? "

" You mean Lady Macdonald," said Dr. Harriman, supplying the point immediately desired to this very vague acquaintance with Canadian current history and dignities. " Doubtless, I shall see Sir John and herself in public. I do not expect to visit at Earnscliffe. As to the carnival, that comes later, I think. But there is always winter pleasure, — sledging, tobogganing. One is sure of those things."

"You'll go tobogganing at Rideau! They say that is so *perfectly gorgeous!* Winter must be fine in Canada. I think I should respect it there; it means something, and holds to its intention. You know what to reckon on. Our climate is simply exasperating. The cold snaps are vicious, and the thaws are weakly contemptible."

"It is of an uncertain temper, truly; and perhaps one can bear steady cold better than freakish alternations. But I cannot bear it always. I am feeble enough to be glad of a thaw now and then, just for consolation. If one can only be reminded that a real balminess may come some time, one can wait."

Dr. Harriman was dividing counters for a new round game, as he spoke. He placed a little heap before Rill Raye, next whom he had secured a seat. He leaned a little toward her, so doing, and it seemed as if his words, in that movement, fell especially to her. But she took no notice at all. She picked up her counters, one by one, carefully verifying their number, and presently the game went on.

There was a prize to be contested for, and certain conditions, at each deal, put one player out.

It was narrowed down at last to Dr. Harriman and
Cyrilla. So long as she held cards, he played his
best; if she had failed, he would have "died," I
believe, at the next hand. It turned out as he had
hoped ; they were left to finish the game against
each other.

Dr. Harriman dealt. A winning card came
into Rill's hand. She laid the whole before him,
face up, upon the table, seeming to decide the result. There was a little shout. " Rill has won!"
they said. " Give it to her, Dr. Harriman."

That was what he had played for. It was a
pretty bangle. " May I put it on ? " he asked.

" It is not mine at all," Rill said, quietly, and
rose up from her seat. " That was *your* card, Dr.
Harriman. You misdealt it."

He knew what she meant, though it had not
been a misdeal, in count. He had more skill than
that. It was awkward ; what could he do with the
thing, if Rill would not take it? And Rill, with
no least emphasis of manner, had moved just far
enough away to be out of the scene. She was
speaking now, very simply, to Sue Wilder.

" You will have to keep it yourself, Miss Connie," Dr. Harriman said, holding it out to the
hostess.

" I will not be fettered, either," replied Connie,
laughing, and tossing her hands behind her, though

he had not asked to put it on. " We will try for it another time. It is great fun," she added. The doctor bowed with a profound gravity, and laid the trinket on the table.

" Even a Canadian winter has its spring, Miss Raye. Do you always mean to be like this ? "

It was Dr. Harriman, who met and stopped her half way on the staircase, hat in hand. She was coming down to Clementhy, who waited for her at the door.

" I don't know," said Rill. " I mean," she went on with a resolve, and her smile was like the sun on crystal — " I mean to be always pleasant, if I can. But I must be clear and true."

" And icy cold," said Dr. Harriman.

" I am very warm — in my friendships, Dr. Harriman," the girl returned.

" Then be friends with me ! It is all I ask for — now."

" You need not ask it. We are not unfriends. Good-night. I must go down."

" May I walk to the cottage with you ? "

" I thank you. I have Clementhy. Aunt Amelia sends her because she prefers it. Good-night." She held out her hand, reaching it from under the warm, light white wrap that folded her head and shoulders like a wreath of snow.

" I told you I could not *bear* continued freezing!" said the doctor, in an emphatic undertone, as he caught the hand in his with a significant strength, and turned with her upon the stairs. She released it with as much decision.

"Then you should not go to Canada," she answered, lightly.

"I would go to — everlasting flames — for you!" he muttered, looking after her as she vanished out upon the porch.

But he could not stand there, upon the staircase. He turned his hat in his hand, looking into it as if to make certain of his own, and then went down, as feet and voices came hurrying along behind him.

Putnam King was wise and brave; he stayed away from Wewachet. He meant to come once in a while, but not now. He was in earnest to work; to prove himself; to make this very first winter declare something. Then, perhaps — But, meanwhile, he would not seek to advance his claim with Rill, and he certainly would not himself occupy, or place her in, an equivocal position.

So the weeks went by, on into December. Miss Haven went into town, to stay during the busy ante-Christmas with the Rextells. She had all her buying and putting up to do for the beautiful Noeltide giving.

She did not give quite like other people. It was her entertaining-time, she said; she gave no par-

ties, she made no festivals; so she remembered,
and complimented, and bestowed, now. Her
equals, and those better off, in worldly goods, she
complimented; she sent dainty little remembrances,
which cost no great deal and were easily dispatched; to the poor she gave substantially, and
in conscientiously large proportion; but it was to
a certain sort — not always most judiciously or
carefully or generously considered — that she gave
with most thought and distinction.

People who could not be "bestowed upon" at
other times; to venture just the right thing with
whom, for their delight or want, only Christmas
gave gracious opportunity; it was to them that the
most ingeniously adapted gifts went with the nicest
detail, and the keenest pleasure in the formal ar-
rangement. Exquisitely tied-up boxes, whose very
tint was a harmony with their contents; quaint
and curious baskets; cases of permanent use and
value and ornament, — these were the outside;
within, the happy recipients found things each had
been doing without and secretly longing for, —
beautiful pictures; soft, rich rugs; a whole set of
books by some beloved author; a shawl; a bit of
delicate household adorning; perhaps, for an invalid, some express furnishing or contrivance for
special comfort, or material for pleasant work;
novelty of patterns, bundles of wools and silks and

plushes ; perhaps, to some young girl, a pretty
gown even, with blessed privilege of " Chryst-
messe " freedom ; whatever the year had brought
to her watchful knowledge as the thing best suited,
most likely to be welcomed with a joy. And all
this took time, and much work, beforehand. So
she and the Rextells, grown toward each other in
their heart-regard and common purposes, were together in the city for this loveliest of carnivals, —
these holy days before the calendar holiday.

And Rill was left, just now — as to her most
real companionships — a good deal alone.

CHAPTER XXII.

TWO LETTERS.

DR. HARRIMAN had bided his time. He had fully resolved what next to do, but he would choose his opportunity. It had come now, when apparently there was a temporary end to interfering, superseding things. A pause and gap which might show to Cyrilla Raye, as it showed to his own limited and mistaken discernment, that nothing was very permanent to her here, of interest and connection with people whose prior places and claims were elsewhere. He thought he divined astutely. He wrote her a letter.

Cyrilla took it from the office one day with other matters for her aunt. The first glance at the hand-writing startled her. It was one she did not know; a fine manly chirography. Could it be? —

But the blue stamp in the corner rebuked her hasty foolishness. It was a local drop-letter. She put it in her pocket with a crumple, blushing furiously all to herself for her own half thought, and at the other perchance which obtruded itself, in a vexation both subjective and objective. She had got to read it, she supposed.

At home, and in her own room, she drew it forth, reluctantly.

" My dear Miss Raye," it began. " I can no longer bear your misunderstanding of me. I must at least beg your fairer judgment, before I dare ask anything beyond. I did neither you nor myself justice when I talked with you that day at Shepaug. I should have said more or less. That I said anything was — you must surely perceive — because there was growing so much to be said that some time I should inevitably speak. It has been growing ever since, through all your coldness and avoidance. I love you. I loved you then, and therefore I told you of my life. I wished you to know what lay in my way, and that it was in the way of that which I most dearly wished. If I had asked you that day to wait with me — for me — would you have waited ? I ask you now. I beseech it of you with all my heart. I desire, I need you, as I need my soul's salvation. Life holds nothing else for me that I can work or wait for. If you can quite forgive me, — if you can say to me some little word of hope, — write me the briefest answer, and I will be very glad and grateful. But do not write me ' No.' Do not put that in irrevocable black and white. If you hesitate, if you even mean refusal, now, keep it back, and leave me with such hope as I had before. I will presume upon nothing ; but I will never cease to endeavor to deserve and win you.   ROBERT HARRIMAN."

This was explicit enough. This was ardent enough. It was terrible enough to a young girl who had never had such a letter written to her before ; never heard such words of eager desire spoken ; never dreamed what they could be.

Had she drawn it upon herself ? Had there been what might seem "tactics," as Connie Norris had accused her ? Had it been as if she would have all this or nothing ? And how could she answer the " No," that he begged her not to write ? Must she not write, and say how impossible it was ? Could she encourage, even by that silence which was a mere withholding of the " no " ?

And yet, what should she say to him ? What was it that made the impossibility so positive, — the thing he was so willing to wait for, so certainly nowhere in the farthest future ever to be ready for him ?

All these questions rushed upon her. They sent the blood in quick leaps of affright and shame and resistance to her face and her fingers' ends ; then they caught it back again to her heart, as she sat pale, quiet, only conscious of one thing, that the answer, now or ever, was " No " — almost fiercely, " *No ! No !* "

Miss Bonable's mail had included that big envelope which came to her twice a year through the hands of her Boston broker; that important package which she always received silently, safely locked away, and in consequence of which made very shortly afterwards her long day's visit to the city.

She came, from the examination and careful bestowal of this, into Rill's room. Rill sat still with the letter on her lap. She had thrust it back into the envelope. She did not know what to do with it. She wished it would disappear, that she might not have to touch it again, to dispose of it in any way.

" Who is your letter from, Cyrilla? " demanded her aunt, very naturally, since Cyrilla did not get a great many letters.

The girl looked up bravely. " It is a note from Dr. Harriman, aunt Amelia," she said.

" *Him?* What does he write notes for? What does he want? Are you going to answer it? "

" I do not think it quite requires an answer. It was to tell me something. Besides," she added, " he is going away. No, I shall not write to him."

" I should hope not. I have n't any opinion of Dr. Harriman, — not any at all! "

Cyrilla could not help smiling at the positiveness of the negation. " It seems to me you have, auntie," she said. " And I don't think you are quite fair to him. He is a gentleman."

"May be. There are different sorts. He ain't *my* sort, and he knows it. I should like to know what he says to you that you don't mean to answer."

"If I did, auntie, I would tell you all about it. Where were your letters from ?"

She spoke, not with the old, cool defiance, but with a frank, sweet assertion of her independence. Composure had returned to her, with the diversion to her aunt of immediate consideration ; putting by, and determining in the instant of reply to her, all question of what to do as to Dr. Harriman. In what she could but say to Miss Bonable's catechising, she had answered herself.

"I don't know as it's your place to inquire," Miss Bonable said to the counter question, with her old curtness.

Rill had not thought of retort, or intrusion; she had simply changed the subject. Miss Bonable walked out of the room with her chin up.

"Now I have offended her," said Rill to herself, "and I am sure I did not mean to." Nevertheless, the little side issue had been a relief.

Two days after, Miss Bonable went to town, for the first time in nearly three months. She had a good deal to do ; there were the safety vault, and the bank, and the broker, to be visited ; there would have to be a long talk about investments, and a settling of the fresh commissions ; then she would go to her old friend who lived in rooms in Grackle Place, and lunch and rest with her; it would be late, as usual, when she would return.

At the station, she caught sight of Dr. Harriman. He came in with Colonel Sholto.

" So you are off to Canada, I hear?" she heard the colonel say; and Dr. Harriman answer, " Not to-day; to-morrow, possibly."

She simply thought, in the same style that she might have spoken, — " Humph! A good riddance enough. Should n't care if he would go to Jerusalem, and stay there!"

Why she so intensely disliked Dr. Harriman she scarcely could have told; but she was to remember those two chance sentences; they were to have more significance for her to-morrow.

Rill had the day before her; so had Clementhy Pond. For dinner, Rill would find her own lunch; she always did when Miss Bonable was away. The pantry held plenty; there was always rich, sweet milk; Rill liked to take a little tray of her own arranging to her room, and sit down with it, and a book beside her. She was one of those persons who recognize by an instinct of special comfort, how we are fed in more ways than one, and how pleasantly mental and bodily hunger may be appeased together.

Miss Pond was secluded in her bedroom over

the kitchen. She was "hooking" a rug; this long day of liberty was a treat to her. She was cutting up long strips of bright yellow flannel, and snipping them off in little rectangles, into a basket. She was going to work a huge sunflower into her pattern. She had never heard of Oscar Wilde; she knew nothing of the prescriptions of æsthetics; it was her own inspiration.

Miss Bonable had gone early. An hour or two later one of the depot drivers, coming up for Mrs. Rospey, had stopped at the cottage with letters from the morning mail. One, this time, for Clementhy Pond, and another, again, for Cyrilla. With Clementhy's we have no interest, save that it helped to keep her yet more strictly immured and occupied, and that Cyrilla was left yet more entirely to what the day might be to her.

It was a queer little letter that had come to her. She turned it over with a puzzled surprise, before she opened it. There was a yellow, queen's-head postage-stamp, to begin with; it had started from the British Dominion, somewhere; then it had traveled, blunderingly, hither and yon, about the United States, for a month at least, by various dates. It was scrawled all over with strange names. It had been to two or three Newmarkets — one away in Missouri; to a Menasket, a Winiskit, a Nonatick; it had "try" this, that and the other in red and black and blue crossings. At last it had come to Wewachet, and Rill's hands.

She broke it open. Like some explosion from an infernal machine, the thing she read in it shattered her whole life as she had known it. Rent, blasted, the circumstance that had been about her, all fact that she had believed of herself was torn from its foundations and sent hurling over her head. Before her lay a chasm. Behind her was impassable wreck and barrier. Nothing could be as it had been, ever again. Instead, what should be? At first, in her confusion, she could hardly think.

With all her difficult peculiarity, she had always thought Miss Bonable a just woman. But what terrible injustice was this that she had done? How had she hidden truth and separated lives?

One thing cleared itself from the chaos of her thought, — she could not stay here ; she could not confront aunt Amelia with this, or ask of her. How could she believe anything that she might choose to say about it? Aunt Amelia had kept Rill's whole real life from her all these years. She could not even bear to see her again. And, another thing, she must go to the writer of this letter. For the writer was her mother.

She was poor ; she was ill ; she was in a little " House of Mercy " hospital in Montreal, — " Mai-

son de Sainte Espérance." She had had years of
trouble and struggle; she had been alone; she had
no friends. She would not say she had been wise,
or good, herself; she had been very foolish and
wrong. But they had never trusted her. If they
had — if she had been happy — if it had not been
for Miss Bonable — " Amelia, your aunt," the letter said — it might have been all different; she
might have stayed; she might have had the care
and comfort of her little child. She had been so
young. But they had never made allowance; they
had never had patience. They had driven her off;
they had taken away her little child. Amelia had
hated her. She had watched and suspected her,
always. She had loved Rill's father, who had gone
away to the other end of the world. He was a rich
man, now; he was sending home money, she was
sure, to this child that Amelia had got from her;
Amelia had got everything. But now the child
was grown, was a woman; she could choose; she
might at least come to her mother, who could not
come to her; she might let her tell her story, which
had been kept back, or, may be, told wrong; she
might let her see the little girl that she had lost so
long.

And there the letter ended. It asked nothing
but that Rill should come. But beyond that, there
was a claim, a care. There was money. Rill could

do for her what she pleased, if this were true. That was all left unsaid; nothing had ever been said till now, in this sore need and longing.

Rill could not know how that had been; that in this little way-off hospital, to the woman lying there, dependent, after all her life of selfishness and error, upon the ministry of these good Gray Sisters, had come, by chance, among miscellaneous reading for the inmates, an Australian newspaper; that in it had been mention of some new great enterprise, in which leading men at Adelaide were engaged; foremost among them "the well-known house of Raye & McLeod;" with personal tribute to Marcus Raye, Esq., the head of the firm, and president of the new corporation.

Yes, there was undoubtedly money; she knew Marcus Raye would not neglect to provide generously for his child; and his child was hers. *Hinc illæ lacrimæ;* hence this pull upon the old chord of mother-love and yearning that had been slack and unthrilled so long.

To Cyrilla, it was like a word out of another existence, one that she had died from and missed knowledge of. However she was to find her, whatever she was to learn of her, she must go to her mother. Undoubtedly, in this she was still Cyrilla; the rash, wild impulsiveness of her nature was asserting itself; she would be doing but a half-judged thing.   But who was there to help her?

Miss Haven?   If she had been right there — but in this convulsion, this cataclysm of her life, how was she to go to her?   All things were changing for her; all things were thrown into a whirl and seethe from which nothing could come out as it had been.   How was she to go with this to the aunt of Putnam King?   The most beautiful force that had entered into the world of her experience was now impelling her away; away from all that could never be again.

And it was not two months yet since Halloween.

CHAPTER XXIII.

RILL'S RUBICON.

" WHATEVER it was, whoever had been to blame, I had a right to know. It was my life. I had a right to live it, or at least to have been ready ! " Rill cried out to herself bitterly. " A father and a mother at the two ends of the earth ! Oh, it was cruel, it was wicked, to keep it back from me, and let it come like this ! Your own sister, too, *Miss Bonable !*" she broke forth, with almost an absurdity of indignation, as if confronting her aunt Amelia with the charge, and flinging at her the hard name that thrust off kindred. " You ought to have followed her ; you ought to have found her, and stood by her ! You had me to help you, — the little child ! She would have come back for me, and I should have had my mother ! You had no right to keep me, and to let her go ! I *never* can forgive you — and I was just beginning to think I loved you ! "

After this storm swept through and over her — she did not know how long it lasted ; one cannot

measure a cyclone while in it — she sat down, quite
still, for a space, and let her way show itself before
her. She did not try to make a plan ; she looked
on in a sort of blankness, while the plan made
itself.

She must go to Montreal. She must find, she
must see, this mother. " Come to the Maison de la
Sainte Espérance," the letter said. " It is in street
Larmes des Anges. Ask for Mother Marthe
or Sister Véronique. Tell them you belong to
me and I have sent for you. You need not tell
them everything. Only come and just say that
till I have talked with you. May be you don't believe me but you will. Then you can say what you
like afterward."

This was the way it was written, in short periods,
evading clauses and commas. It was well spelled,
and fairly expressed, throughout, but evidently
not the work of one easily practiced. It was
signed " E. B. Raye." The woman had honest
right to both the initial letters, though she had
always been called " Loraine." Spelled out in full,
the Christian name was Eloraine : one of those
curious fancy constructions that are found in country town records, and in remote old graveyards.
But she had doubtless remembered in writing it,
that Miss Bonable's sister was " Esther," and had
shrewdly divined the ambiguity or absolute igno-

rance in which Cyrilla might have been left. She
would have come across Esther Bonable's name,
she guessed; and Amelia was "aunt Amelia" to
her.

It was well guessed and ventured. Cyrilla knew
and secretly cherished the name she believed to
have been her mother's. "Why was n't I named
for my mother?" she had startled Miss Bonable
once by asking. "Esther is a strong, sensible
name; perhaps I should n't have been so flighty if
I had n't been called Cyrilla."

"You were called after your father's mother,"
Miss Bonable had answered, shortly. "And *she*
was a stiddy, reliable woman."

There she had dropped the bar that always fell
across any talk of former things or relations. Silence, withdrawal, or determined change of subject,
ended inevitably all approach to investigation, and
Rill was afraid of what there might be to hear.

Now, she knew. Now, there was one thing certain. She must go to Montreal. Nobody must
hinder her. Something of effort, of courage required, gave a stimulus, if not exhilarating, at least
counteractive to her real trouble; it met her temperament, always roused to whatever called for decision, daring. It was a long journey; it was winter; she was all alone; she must venture everything, without advice, at once, and by herself. Per-

haps a less demand would have given her less determination.

She went to her little bureau drawer, that was under the glass. There were fifty dollars here, of her last rent. It was to have bought her a new cloak and dress. Never mind that, now. She had two hundred more laid by, at the New England Trust Company. She could get that, and if there were more, rightly belonging to her, as this letter said, and as was likely if all the rest it said were true, Miss Bonable would send it to her. Miss Bonable was a — no, she could never say again that she was a just woman; but she would not cheat in money. Rill would be able to help her mother; when she had found her, they would think together what to do. Something hardened up in her against any other hope she had ever had. It was no use looking that way; it was like Lot's wife. She would be petrified: she would be changed into utter bitterness and deadness, if she did. She must just go straight on.

She brought carefully and quietly downstairs into the unused north parlor, a small square trunk. She carried and put into it the things she needed for a journey. Clementhy came to her at lunch time, or after, — Rill did not know which, for she had not remembered her own little tray, and her book, and her quiet pasturing of mind and body, at

all. Clementhy came and said she guessed she
would walk over to Shepaug. She could be back
before Miss Bonable. Her brother-in-law would
fetch her home. "Very well," Rill told her.
"Lock your end of the house; I will lock the
front. I shall go down to the village."

So she did; she wrote a note first to Miss
Haven, inclosing with it a little blue book and
a check which she drew to Miss Haven's order.
"She will do that for me, I know," she said.

At the post-office she had the parcel registered,
and mailed it; then she bought a small can of
sweet biscuits and some oranges; she did not feel
as if she could eat Miss Bonable's bread again;
she stopped at the express office, and ordered them
to send up presently and take a trunk from the cottage to the station; these things accomplished, she
hastened back to Brook Lane, sent off her box
when the man came for it, and wrote one more
note, a very brief one.

How she got rid of the hours that remained, she
hardly knew; she waited till she heard Clementhy
below again, then she called to her and told her she
was tired and had a headache and would not come
down to tea. She would go to bed, she thought.

When Miss Bonable came back, Rill's bedroom
door was locked, and she made neither sign nor
sound in answer to the knock and question that

were tried quietly once, and not repeated. Miss Bonable was tired, herself; it was seven o'clock; it seemed a long evening already; she went to bed, and the winter night and stillness fell down upon them all.

It was yet in the twilight of the December morning when Rill, with her shawl and her hand-satchel, and her brown veil tied close down across her face shielding from cold and observation, walked over the mile of road, clean crusted with smooth-worn snow. She took a train half an hour earlier than was needful, that she might be less likely to meet any acquaintances, and be fairly away before any one at home would be stirring to miss her. She found her trunk at the station, had it checked and put upon the platform, and stood there by it when, three minutes later, the electric signal rang, and the engine came steaming around the curve from Shepaug. The sun came up red over the marshes, as the train slipped through the river cut, sped on between the woods, and rushed out along the line that shot its level, glittering parallels toward the city whose roofs and spires shone presently in sight upon its clustered hills, and out over the great suburban avenues.

It was morning, bringing new things everywhere; how new and strange to thousands of lives only each of the glad or anxious or suffering thousands could tell. Rill wondered if it could mean as much to anybody else as to herself. To aunt Amelia? Oh, yes! She thought of her with a pang of wronged, angry tenderness ; but how could she herself have done otherwise than she had done ? It was aunt Amelia who was responsible ; it was she who had shaped things to the issue ; the very yearning and regret Rill felt sprang from that in her which would not have let her stay and face Miss Bonable with the reproach of her doing ; neither could she have borne a contradiction of her purpose. She must do this, and she must do it alone. She must find her mother, whatever came of it.

And suppose she did not find her ? Very well ; that possibility had nothing to do with it ; it was her duty to try.

At the Boston station she bought her ticket, got her check, engaged a seat in the parlor car, and had a cup of hot coffee and a roll at the café ; then she went into the train and found her place in the Pullman. She sat there alone for some minutes ; it was still early ; she leaned back in the deep chair and shut her eyes ; it was her first pause in the rush of needful action. She was tired ; she did not wish to look at the movement about her, up and down the platform ; luggage being hurried by on trucks ; groups of friends, gayly talking,

happy in all starting off together; other groups
bidding good-by and parting.

People began to come in behind her; she sat
still, and did not look around; her chair was near
the front. By and by the train gave a slow, heavy
pull, the great wheels measured the lengths of rail
with separate clanks; the engine panted; then it
got easy, regular breath; the rails were clicked off
faster under the smoother, swifter roll; presently
their rapid-running beats pulsed the miles like
minutes; the causeways and the bridges had been
crossed and left behind; the State Prison and Bun-
ker Hill Monument had wheeled away to the right;
they were whizzing by the first suburban stations;
they were out into the white frozen country.

Charles River was Rill's Rubicon; she had
passed it. Aunt Amelia had her note by this time;
she was off beyond recall.

She shut her eyes again; she tried to shut out
thinking; and she went to sleep. Poor child! she
had not really rested all the night.

Somebody had taken a seat upon the opposite
side, a little back; he had laid a rug and satchel
and his Railway Guide upon it, and had gone away
into the smoker.

Nearly an hour went by; he had returned to his
place; but of the little figure over across, nothing
was visible as it still leaned hidden, with its veiled

face turned away. Only a fold of dark blue winter serge that fell to the floor from around the heavy curving arm of the chair, gave evidence of its occupant. The two who were to be all-day neighbors had not seen each other yet.

They were speeding away along the reaches of the Merrimack, whose narrowing current made its darkly vivid rush between the snowy ice-floes, when Rill was roused by the conductor's deferent touch and request for ticket. Swinging slightly round upon her revolving seat, as he passed on, she put up her veil and glanced across through the opposite windows upon the white slopes of hills that just then shut in the valley, wondering what part of the country it might be.

The gentleman upon the other side put down his newspaper, as the official came to him in turn; he saw, past the shoulder of the man, the sweet, strong profile suddenly thrown in view. He hurriedly took back his ticket, and started to his feet. The conductor moved along, and the passenger went forward; he remembered just in time to stay his step from a spring, and to tone his voice from others' hearing.

"Miss Raye!"

Cyrilla looked quickly up; she found herself face to face with Dr. Harriman.

We must leave them there; I must tell you meanwhile about Miss Bonable.

At this very moment, or nearly so, she was ringing Mrs. Rextell's bell on Mount Vernon Street.

CHAPTER XXIV.

EXACTLY LIKE MRS. REXTELL.

A GRAY-HAIRED, black-coated, severely respecta-
ble servant opened the door. He was the town
butler; he did not know Miss Bonable, who asked
to see Miss Haven. "The ladies are all out," he
told her.

"Then, if you please, I must come in and wait,"
Miss Bonable said, with her usual curt decision.
"I am Miss Bonable, from Wewachet. I have an
important errand to Miss Haven."

The butler civilly threw back the door, and
stood aside. The servants in this house were
always civil.

"Will you walk into the little reception parlor,
Miss Bonable, and sit down?" the man asked her;
and then he went and called the lady's maid. He
might be civil; but he was duly cautious, also.

Agnes was always with her mistress, here or
there. She knew Wewachet. Agnes came. The
poor lady by this time was faint with worry, effort,
disappointment; she sat bolt upright against the

back of a tall chair, looking as if otherwise she would sway and fall.

Agnes hastened to her. "Miss Bonable," she said, " you are not well. You must have something. Melcombe, bring a glass of wine."

" I came in without my breakfast," said Miss Bonable, moving her lips nervously ; she meant to smile. " I was in a hurry."

" Bring a biscuit, and some cold chicken, Melcombe," added Agnes to her order.

The girl was kind, by nature and by training. She was also a little fond of representing her mistress with authority, strong in the certainty of what her mistress would approve. " And then you must come upstairs, Miss Bonable," she said. She was truly fine in her assumption of responsibility, and her calm indorsement of Miss Bonable's correctness. Melcombe obeyed her directions, and stood meekly aside.

So when Mrs. Rextell and her guest returned from their morning drive and charity meeting, they found Miss Bonable on the sofa in the dressing-room between their sleeping-chambers ; outwardly quiet, but holding herself there by main force. She sprang up as they entered.

" Oh, have we waked you ? " asked Mrs. Rextell, regretfully, and quite as if she had come home expecting to find her country neighbor there asleep.

" I have n't been asleep. I have been in a stun these three hours," answered Miss Bonable. " A terrible thing has happened, Miss Haven; Rill has gone away."

After she had spoken these words, in a kind of mechanical dullness, Miss Bonable dropped herself back upon the sofa, and put her hands over her face. " I ain't angry ; and I can't cry," she said.

" I will leave you with her ; if I can do any good, call me," whispered Mrs. Rextell gently, and went into her own room, closing the door.

" I don't understand. Rill gone away ? When ? where ? " asked Miss Haven. But first she sat down by Miss Bonable, and put her hand upon her friend's shoulder. leaning her own face tenderly close to hers. Miss Bonable drew round, freeing herself, not ungently, but as one who must hold herself up alone.

" She 's gone — to Canada. And Dr. Harriman 's gone. Now you know it all."

" My dear friend, I don't know anything ; except that that cannot be true — unless as two separate facts. Do explain."

" It is n't separate. *That* explains." And she pushed a paper, folded and rolled, and pinched and clenched small, into Miss Haven's hand. Miss Haven opened it from its many creases and read this : —

"I am going away. I am sorry, but it cannot
be helped. You will guess what I have gone for.
If you had trusted me, if you had let me understand my own life, if you had tried to believe any
good of my — the person I am going to, it might
have been different. There might never have been
any going away at all. I could not tell you, I
could not ask you, now; it is my own concern, my
own decision; it had to be. I will send you some
word from Montreal."

Miss Bonable gazed straight into Miss Haven's
face while she read; as if through her face, into
her thought, she would reach to read something
that she had not been able of herself to find in the
lines.

Miss Haven lifted her eyes when she had finished, and met the look. "What she says is true;
you have not trusted her."

"Oh, I meant to! When I had got her where
I could! I was trying to bring her up to *be*
trusted!" broke in quick exclamations from Miss
Bonable's lips.

"You have been too long bringing her up,"
Miss Haven said quietly, using the very word Rill
had used so long ago. "Begin by trusting her
now."

"Now! When it is all over? When she has
gone away with that — oh!" Miss Bonable could

not put the final word; she could not, after all, accuse Rill in that outright speech.

" Nothing is over. And she has not done what you think."

" What else can she have done ? "

" Don't you see ? She never would have written you this had it been — Dr. Harriman. Dr. Harriman may have gone to Canada; it is an unfortunate coincidence ; but I am sure that it has nothing to do with Rill. She did not remember that, when this came on her suddenly. Miss Bonable, it is a quite different thing. Rill has heard from her mother."

" Through *you* ? " Miss Bonable demanded quickly, at that statement.

" No, my friend. I wish she had. I had not told her. Mrs. Raye " —

" Hush ! There *is* no Mrs. Raye ! "

" Rill's mother must be in Montreal. She must have written."

For a minute Miss Bonable held her breath.

" Do you think *that* ? " she said at last.

" I do. I think it is like Rill — impetuous, hasty, noble — to have gone right off to her."

Again Miss Bonable sat silent, breathless.

Mrs. Rextell knocked upon her side of the dressing-room door. " May I come in ? " she asked. " I have a note for you. It has just been brought to me.   It may explain," she added as she entered.

It was Rill's note to Miss Haven.

"I am going away," it said.   "I must.   Something I never knew before — a duty — has come to me.   I will write and tell you more when I understand more myself.   I know you will believe in me,, and that you will do for me what I have to ask you.   I shall want money, — whatever really belongs to me.   I hardly know what that may be. I shall have to leave it to you to ask ; I am sure it will be all right.   I send a check for what I had of my very own ; it is to your order.   Will you get it, and send it to me in a draft, or whatever way is right and regular, as soon as you have received my address ?   Good-by, dear Miss Haven.   I am sorry, *sorry*, for everybody.   But my whole life is changed, and I cannot help it."

Those last sentences were very full, as Miss Haven read them, between the syllables.   There was a message in them for Miss Bonable, though Rill had not been able to write her name.   There was something in them also that reached beyond Miss Bonable, to what that excellent person, with all her watchfulness, had never discerned — for the very reason that it was not a thing to be afraid of, but a thing of good.

"It is just as I expected.   Rill has certainly heard from her mother."

Miss Bonable's eyes grew wide in amazement, turning from Miss Haven to Mrs. Rextell, as these words were uttered.

"Mrs. Rextell knows. She will help us," said Miss Haven, to the look. " I did tell *her*, long ago, out of honor and love to you, Miss Bonable. I ought to have told Rill ; but I waited. I have never been sorry for telling too much; it is the telling too little that always does harm."

" But, Miss Haven, it is a terrible thing any way. It is n't explainable. She 's gone ; and he 's gone ; and folks will never believe. And what will become of her — off there — with that woman ? "

" Folks will always have to believe the truth. And the truth will be that Rill has gone on a journey, and is in the care of friends, as she ought to be. I will go to Montreal myself."

" They will think they see through that ; even if you bring her home again." Poor Miss Bonable, who " would have made a pretty good burglar herself," was so swift in devising malevolent possibilities.

Mrs. Rextell had been reading Rill's note, which Miss Haven had put into her hand. Now she spoke.

" Let *me* go to Montreal," she said. " Everybody knows I am like a bird on a perch, always ready for a flitting. And why should I not invite

Miss Raye to go with Margaret and me? I do invite her. We will be there with her to-morrow night. Miss Bonable, you will stay here on a little visit with Miss Haven, please, and just get rested and quiet, until you hear from us. Then, if it seems best, you can go home, and report facts. I hope Miss Haven will not leave until after we return. That may be very soon, you know."

Miss Haven's eyes glistened. "This is so exactly like you, that I might have expected it," she said. "But we shall have to wait for the address; you can hardly set off to-morrow morning."

"Oh, well, we will just wait and see. Agnes shall have us ready. And now all you have to do is to cheer each other up. Don't you want to send some word to Wewachet, Miss Bonable? Let your woman know you will be away a day or two — you and Miss Rill — then she will have something proper to say. Oh, it will all work beautifully; things always do, when you mean right, and can get just a little ahead of them!'"

Mrs. Rextell laughed. She had a gleeful way of undertaking things; a sufficient reason for undertaking a great deal, unexpectedly — a chance to help somebody — always made her merry. "It was so good and wise of you to tell me all about it," she said to Miss Haven. "I have understood you and Cyrilla for a long time, Miss Bonable, better than you have understood each other ; but perhaps I could n't have taken the whole right in now, in a hurry."

" What will Clementhy have said already ? " asked Miss Haven.

Mrs. Rextell laughed.

" Oh, I know what you are thinking of," Miss Haven replied to that, serenely. " But I am not inconsistent. There 's a time to keep silence, and a time to speak."

" She won't have said anything, except that we have both gone to Boston. Clementhy Pond is still. She is n't a chattering brook," said Miss Bonable.

Certainly the dear lady was beginning to be more comfortable in her mind. Before, then, anything else occurs to her as disastrously possible, we will leave her with these good friends in Mount Vernon Street, and go back to Rill on board the northward-speeding train.

CHAPTER XXV.

THE TELEGRAM.

It had not occurred to one of these friends, somehow, that Dr. Harriman and Cyrilla could possibly have happened upon this very same train together. That was spared them. They only thought of the two as having gone away within the same twenty-four hours, bound, by distinct routes, to two different points in Canada.

The elements for another little calculation were happily wanting to them also. They did not reckon upon the sharp eyes of Mrs. Porbeagle early at her window; or upon the trained acuteness of Sam Porbeagle, floor-walker at one of the big stores, who had gone in by the train which Rill had taken; nor upon the curiosity and comment of half a dozen village folk, about the station'; nor the knowledge of several fellow-passengers by the 7.30, that Dr. Harriman had set off at that time; nor upon the note of Miss Bonable's own pale face and anxious look as she followed by the forenoon shopping train.

Beyond all, they did not remember that it was the afternoon of the Benevolent Circle at the church parlors, where they would make patchwork quilts, and quilt together patchwork items such as these, that might be picked up of the absent, and brought in ; in both pieces of work, the skill and value being in the smallness of the bits that could nevertheless be cleverly joined into a brilliant pattern.

Dr. Harriman, meeting Rill in this surprising manner, remembered at once a dozen such possibilities. He was alive instantly to the position of things, and to the aspect it might take at Old Village. It was to his honor that his first anxiety was for Rill. Had she come from home this morning ? Had she come alone ? What could possibly be her errand and destination, upon this long express ? The first two questions he put to her. Yes ; she had come alone ; from home ; she was going a journey.

" Might he ask, was it far ? Miss Bonable ? " —

" Miss Bonable did not know, Dr. Harriman."

Rill made this straightforward, amazing answer, with her eyes looking clearly and unafraid into his. It was an assertion of absolute right and sufficient reason ; with a brevity and reticence which said that her purpose and her secret were her own.

" But — if you will forgive me "— and he took

the vacant chair beside her, turning it to a conversational angle with her own.   There were but few
passengers ; the others were all below the middle
of the car.   " It is a strange coincidence, our being
here ; and — are you sure you can quite manage?
Might I not do something for you ? "

" It is strange," Rill said, still in that contained
and certain way.   " I do not wonder you should
think so.   No — I thank you, Dr. Harriman — I
need nothing done for me."

" But why ?   Forgive me ! " he said again.   " I
wish you would tell me more.   I think your errand
must be a very serious one ; and — are you sure "—
he finished this time what he had been on the point
of saying before, and had turned aside from — " are
you sure it will be rightly understood ? "

" I never have been rightly understood ; and *I*,
oh, *I* have understood nothing ! "

Her measured manner broke ; she uttered the
words impulsively.   Then she collected herself with
a visible withdrawal.   " It is a family matter ;
nothing I can tell, or explain ; it is something quite
my own, that I never knew of before.   I am going
to a relative, Dr. Harriman.   I shall not be alone
when I get to Montreal."

She was going all the way, then !   They were
both going all the way, together.   What should he
do with her ?   How could he leave her to herself,

and what could her mysterious errand be? Above
all, what would be imagined or believed at home?
He thought of all the strange conjunctions and dé-
nouements of fiction ; of possible reality that might
be stranger than fiction, more hazardous to this
young girl than she could guess. These family
matters, that have been kept secret while a girl
was growing up; these relatives who turn up and
make claim suddenly,— what were they likely to
be, or to bring with them ? No — he could not
leave her to herself ; but how could he take care of
her ? His heart beat as he thought of a way; of
that for which the opportunity, the excuse, was
thrust before him.

He waited a little while before he spoke again.
Then he said, quite differently, " You did not
answer my letter, Miss Raye."

" Oh, do not speak of that, Dr. Harriman ! I
had forgotten ! "

It was perfectly true that, for the moment, after
the first startle and shock, in the intensity of that
which now occupied her, and concerning which he
questioned her, it had been, as it were, discharged
from her mind. It was such a trivial thing, com-
paratively ; it was so far back, already, in the past
with which she had no more to do.

" My dear Miss Raye! I would not for the
world take any rude or ungenerous advantage ;

but, this wholly unpremeditated circumstance, this
unknown errand which I find you undertaking,
upon what you say yourself is a sudden, brief
knowledge, don't you see how it places me? How
can I let you proceed alone, in what may be a difficulty, an imprudence, for you? And yet, what am
I to do, that might not, in another way, make it
worse? You are so clear and true and single-
hearted, you do not see, you do not guess, what
deception, or danger, may be waiting for you. Or
if you know more than you will tell me — it may
be some trouble, some dread — something or somebody whom it will be self-sacrifice for you to meet
and acknowledge ; there are such things ; you see
I don't know your 'family matters,' as you have
said. If I could meet it with you, whatever it is,
Rill, I am ready ; I am glad! If you will give
me the right to face life with you and for you —
won't you answer me now, Rill, and say that I
may ?"

He leaned toward her, and spoke rapidly and
low ; all his best impulses were in the words and
shaped them ; he looked at her earnestly, with eyes
that might earnestly win a woman ; when he had
spoken he waited gravely for her answer.

She made a slight movement from him as he sat ;
he laid his hand upon the arm of her chair, and
stopped it from turning. "Do not do that," he

said, " people will see ; tell me quietly what you
can tell me ; do not speak hastily ; I can be
patient." He leaned back in his own chair, but
did not take his look away from her.

Rill lifted her eyes. " You mean to be very
generous, and I thank you," she said. " But it is
utterly impossible. I think, if you are kind, you
will let me be by myself. It is all you can do, and
people will see, as you said."

" But you do not see, yourself. Must I say ?
It is not the argument I wish to urge ; but it has
force ; and we must think of it. You say Miss
Bonable does not know."

" I said she did not know. She does, by this
time."

" Everything ? "

" She can guess everything. I did not need to
tell her."

Dr. Harriman paused for an instant, without
reply, from sheer surprise. The absolute single-
ness of purpose, failing to see that any supposition
aside from itself was possible, dismayed him. Then
he said — forced to make suggestion to such inap-
prehensive sincerity : —

" May she not stop short in her guessing ? May
she not be full now of a trouble which only thinks
of you immediately, and of what she fancies may
have concerned you ? Will she guess what you have

kept back? May not all Wewachet be guessing,
by this time — or soon — and guessing wrong?"

Rill remembered the words she had written, and
how she had stinted them. What should Miss
Bonable suppose? She might know nothing about
Montreal, except — what flashed upon her own
mind now. Indignant color swept up into her
face. She was indignant with herself, that she
could guess. "I cannot help it," she said, coldly,
while her cheeks and temples burned.

"I would not urge it," Dr. Harriman repeated;
"but I think of it for you. It urges me. Because
the one thing I can do — best — to serve and pro-
tect you, is the one thing of all the world that I
desire — must that go against me? I want you to
belong to me, Rill; in all circumstances, forever;
for the better or the worse. I will make everything better, if I can. Let it begin now; give me
the power, and let your errand be mine. Let me
help you through it, whatever it is; then I will
take you, my wife, to my sister, my mother. They
will be your mother and sister; it will be for you
as it should be. They will love you; they are
good women, and you will love them."

The color still burned, and even deeper; the
eyes glowed; the eyelids trembled; but she lifted
them, and forced herself to look steadily at him.

"You mean that I should make true the thing

they may think of me, for fear of the thinking?"
she asked, with a pure scorn, not of him, but of the
thing, and the fear. "No, Dr. Harriman; do not
say any more about it. Please, will you go away
now?"

She kept her careful manner, for the outside, her
bravery for the truth-speaking; but she was trembling, he could see, beneath the composure; under
the unswerving lids the tears were shining. He
remembered what was due, and needful; he bowed,
as at casual conversation ended, and withdrew to
his own seat. Not by any means as giving all up,
and leaving her to her own mistake and its complications; but thinking what he could possibly
do for her in the meanwhile that she would not let
him do all he might. He took no refusal, yet, for
himself; he understood the fair pride with which
she repudiated the expedient.

By and by he came and stood quietly at the back
of her chair. She had faced full toward the window, and was sitting motionless, looking forth upon
the white banks and the ice-margin, and the still,
strong current of the river.

"Miss Raye," he said; and she half turned
toward him. "Can you think of *anything* that I
can do for your comfort, or your certainty in any
way?"

"I can think of one thing," she answered him

with the most direct simplicity : " You can go back
to Wewachet; then they will see that there is
nothing to think about." She ordered him as she
had ordered him about the drawing of her tooth;
from the necessity of the case. " You know it
ought to be done," was what she had told him;
and this unhesitant plain speaking put the same
conclusiveness to him to-day.

" I did it, that was all," had been his own word
to Miss Haven. It was all he could afterward
have said of this. But there were other things to
think of first. " Where do you go in Montreal ? "
he asked her. " It will be late, you know."

" To some hotel, at first," she supposed. The
conductor would tell her. She would ask him to
see her safe.

" You had better send a telegram. I will do it
for you, from Concord. I will leave the train
there, and go back to Boston." He knew better
than to add in words, " I will do whatever you
choose and command; I purely desire to serve you."
But he meant that otherwise than in mere words
she should discern it.

" What hotel is there ? " she asked him, with
ingenuous ignorance. There was the St. James,
he told her. Then she wrote a couple of lines upon
a slip of paper, and handed to him with it a dollar
bank-bill from her porte-monnaie. " Will that do ? "
she said.

" It will more than do." And he gave her carefully back two silver quarters.

" I am very grateful to you, Dr. Harriman."
And she held out her hand to him. "Good-by."

" I shall not say good-by to you. I shall never
bid you good-by, Miss Raye." But he left her;
and when the train slowed into the Concord station,
he picked up his valise, threw his coat over his arm,
and walked away among the crowd that swarmed
back and forth along the platforms.

The telegram he sent, however, was not Rill's at
all. It ran this way : —

" Have warm room ready, and carriage at station,
to meet Miss Raye, of Boston, who will arrive by
evening train. Show every care and attention till
friends join her." To this dispatch he appended
with cool audacity the name and address, " Elizabeth Putnam Haven, of Boston."

" They know all the old names, those hotel fel-
lows," he said to himself.

CHAPTER XXVI.

"THE BENEV'."

HE had three hours' waiting in Concord ; then he took an afternoon train back to Boston, where he caught the 5.30 to Wewachet. At seven o'clock he called on Connie Norris. She made to him the same interrogative announcement that half the people he had seen on his way home had done. " Why! you went off this morning, I thought ; " to which he made the same sort of answer, — " I went to town ; I met with a detention ; I am back again. I may not go till next week. Are you sorry? Am I the bad penny ? " etc., etc.

Of course, Connie was delighted. " Now we shall keep you till after the first sociable," she said. " And it's the Benev', to-night, with charades. Won't you come over with me ? "

" I shall be happy to go over with you, certainly ; but I can scarcely stay for the charades. I have something to do — a person to see on business."

" I wish there were n't any business in the world ! " quoth Connie. " Only buzziness."

" Business may have somewhat to do with the buzziness," was the doctor's answer.

She paraded him in, making air and flutter about the door of the hall as they entered. Some heads were turned, and some talk was stopped. Mrs. Porbeagle's voice went on, in a sort of soprano léad, as the chorus softened. " Old Village was pretty lively, I should think, this morning," she had been saying to her inevitable group. " First, Rill Raye off with a trunk, at seven o'clock, for nobody knows where; then, Dr. Harriman off with a valise, at 7.30, for Canada; then aunt Bonable, as mum as a toad and as fidgety inside as a grass-hopper, on the 10.25, sitting with her back to everybody, on the front edge of the front seat of the front car, with her nose run out at the engine to poke it along faster, and scowling at every stop. And she has n't come back yet. Well! I don't know anything, and I don't mean to say anything; but it looks kind o' queer and newsy, and to-be-continued, don't it? I never believed much in that other business. The other aunt tried for that, but she did n't make it out, it seems; *he* has n't been seen in Wewachet this two months; and Miss Abominable was always dead set against the tooth-puller. Well, he 's gone, now, any way; and she 's gone; and she could n't have caught up with her to see her off,— that is, if she needed to start when she did."

Perhaps the tangle of her own unmanageable personal pronouns brought her up; or perhaps it was that in the midst of their eager and irrelevant prancing the partial hush fell suddenly upon the room.

"There he is, this minute!" said young Mrs. Sphyrna Hammerhead, touching Mrs. Porbeagle on the elbow.

"Who? Why! — Dr. Harriman? — It *is n't!* she ejaculated, brokenly, with gasps of astonishment, as the gentleman walked up the room and approached her. "Really, Dr. Harriman, you 're like a ghost! We all thought you were in Canada! Could n't get away from the 'Benevolent,' could you?" she asked, gleaming upon him with her white, large teeth.

"I suppose not, even if I were in Canada," Dr. Harriman responded. "We have the poor always with us; so, I fancy, we shall always have the *benevolent!* No; I did not go to-day. I was prevented."

Even that did not quite checkmate her. "I wonder what it actually all does mean!" she exclaimed, *sotto voce*, to Sphyrna Hammerhead, as he passed on.

He stayed for fifteen minutes in the rooms; drank a cup of coffee; then when the charades were going to begin, he disappeared; took the

7.50 train for town, and rendered himself at Mrs. Rextell's house in Mount Vernon Street, where he asked to see Miss Haven, and told her all the story.

"I used your name," he said; "the whole of it, to be impressive. Now somebody must go to her. If nothing else can be done, I will write to my mother and sister in Ottawa. They will go down. It is only a three hours' run."

"Mrs. Rextell and her daughter will go to-morrow. We only needed the address, and the certainty of her stopping in Montreal."

His errand was accomplished; he got up to go; Miss Haven accompanied him to the door.

"You have done most wisely, most generously, Dr. Harriman. Your sleep should be sweet to-night," she said, upon the threshold, giving him her hand with warmth. He only pressed it, smiled a little curiously, and with bowed leave-taking, went away.

It may not be invariably after our most generous deeds, however, that sleep comes most easily, or is most sweet.

CHAPTER XXVII.

MAISON DE LA SAINTE ESPÉRANCE.

As the day wore on, and the steady rush of the train bore Rill further from home toward the strange, cold north, she had time to realize the irrevocableness of what she had done. She would not change it, if she could; but she perceived its gravity more clearly; and it needed all her brave determination to keep up against a growing sense of loneliness, and a vague stir of apprehension. Up through the wintry stillness of the hills, across the ice-bound rivers, springing or skirting valley-depths where farming villages lay quiet as little cemeteries with their white-roofed barns and dwellings, and idle mill wheels dripped with great stalactites — into the edges of large busy towns, through dreary stations where, in short pause, the scattered wayfarers alighted and embarked — she watched the shifting scenes, and measured both outward distances and the quick, strange experience of the hours. Space and time confused her. *Where was yesterday?*

As far as St. Albans she had the undisturbed monotony of travel. The early dusk had long fallen, and with the shadows loomed misgiving of the night arrival — anxiety about being met and cared for. She could but be thankful for the friendliness that had made probable provision for all this; and she congratulated herself that there would be no trouble of any intermediate move. She sat back in her chair, determined to take such comfort as she could, and one thing at a time; to turn from all disquieting thought of that which was done with, or might be to come.

Suddenly, the porter, who had been very civil all the way, came and laid hand upon her bag and wrap. "We stop here; this car goes no farther," he told her; "I will see you to your place on the other train."

Without time for question she had to follow him, half blindly, through a dimly lighted space from crowded track to track, into a very ordinary and ill-contrasting car indeed. It was half full, and filling up, with men; whatever might be the reason or occasion, they seemed all of one stamp, — a common and disorderly set; a great jabbering of Canadian *patois* was growing clamorous around her; and as she took the seat offered her, she shrank with sudden dismay at perceiving that there was actually no other feminine occupant of the whole carriage.

"Oh, what shall I do?" she exclaimed, involuntarily, to her escort.

"You will be quite safe," was the answer. "It is all right. I expect I may run down on this train myself. I'll look out for you at the door of the car when we arrive." With that, he left her. Whether this was a sudden determination, induced by a promise to Dr. Harriman which that gentleman had made well worth while, or to what peculiar railway arrangements all these strange circumstances were due, I will not undertake to say, and Cyrilla did not conjecture.

It seemed a great while before the train started; something was evidently out of the usual course; when they did move, the boisterous passengers settled into their seats, and she breathed for a time more quietly. She was just reassuring herself in a comparative confidence, when all at once a crash just behind her startled her half way to her feet. Splintered glass and drops of coal oil fell around her; over there, two seats off, the conductor and a passenger were in an angry tussle; every man in the car was up, and hurrying to the point of excitement; all but one old, gray-haired Frenchman, far down toward the front.

"Oh, let me pass!" cried Cyrilla, to those immediately obstructing her; and made her way forward to a place behind the one quiet person.

He turned to her kindly, as she took her seat. "Have no fear, mademoiselle," he said to her. "But what is it that has happened there?"

She began in reply, "I hardly know. I only saw" — when the word was, as it were, snatched from her by a rough voice over her shoulder.

"Oh, you saw, did you?"

Startled, and with sudden foreboding, as the thought flashed swiftly upon her of a police court, evidence, she knew not what, — "Nothing at all, sir!" she answered, with a very determined brevity, and relapsed into a rigid silence, but not for a long time into a real calmness.

Alone, — among such strange fellow - travelers, — the deep night wearing on, — into what had she plunged herself? What next might befall to terrify or endanger her? The gray head before her was her only comfort.

The hours went by in keen endurance; it was very late. The train was overdue; they had lost some time earlier, beside the long delay at St. Albans; bells were clanging for eleven o'clock when they steamed into the murky station-house at Montreal.

Happily and unexpectedly, the porter kept his word; she drew a great breath of thankfulness as his hand reached up to help her at the car-steps.

He went with her through the train-house; found

the badged driver from the St. James; stayed by her through the scramble of the formal, hurried passing of inspection. Then, a moment more, and she was out in the brave, moonlighted air, in an open sledge heaped well with furry robes.

A large, square, corner room, with three great windows and a blazing fire, awaited her; ready service was offered her; a tray, with supper, was brought. She ate and drank, as in some queer phase of a dream, and went to bed.

Early after breakfast the next morning, she asked for a carriage to be called.

" Maison de la Sainte Espérance — Larmes des Anges Street," she said to the driver, who looked down from his box with an odd expression of not surely understanding.

" Larmes des Anges Street! " repeated with authority the hall servant who had obsequiously attended Cyrilla to the carriage door. He had quenched the hackman, but he turned himself to cast a curious glance after the departing equipage, as he went up the broad steps ; and walked straight into the hotel office.

Narrow, steeply sloping, roughly paved streets ; crooked turn ; the fair, open squares left far behind ; mere rims of sidewalk ; old, old houses of all irregular heights and shapes ; crowded sheds, and bits of squalid yard-room ; dirty children, swarming and staring; women's heads, with flapping, broad-frilled caps, thrust forward from doorways, where show was made with stumps of brooms of sweeping off entrances; pails of darksome water thrown out here and there for final service in rinsing down the brick walks to the gutters; everything gave evidence to Cyrilla that she was coming down among the dregs of life over which bright cities build themselves and are gay.

A quieter turn, at last, into a kind of court, where a stinted plot, fenced in, held a few scant trees in the midst; a high-recessed doorway, to which a narrow flight of steps led up; muslin half-blinds at the window; a tin plate, neatly painted, " Maison de la Sainte Espérance."

Cyrilla's heart beat as she rang the bell; a portress, in lay-sister's garb, answered it; Cyrilla asked for Mère Marthe. The Mother was ill. For Sœur Véronique; Sœur Véronique was in retreat.

" Oh, but I must see some one ! " Cyrilla cried, persistent. " I was sent for; it is urgent. I have a friend here, ill; she is — her name is — Raye."

" O—h, it is, then, the poor penitent ! She died, three weeks ago. But I will tell the Mother. Enter, mademoiselle; rest here."

She showed the young girl into a bare, little room; it had for furnishing a wooden table, and four wooden chairs; some prints of the Virgin, and a saint or two, upon the walls ; a yellow cat lying on a window-ledge, blinking great golden eyes.

Presently, a Sister appeared at the doorway.

" Come," she said, and laid her fingers on her lips, as Rill approached. "One does not speak in the corridors," she said, softly ; then turned and led the way.

Several houses had been thrown into one establishment ; there were dark passages, steps up and down ; one long flight, and a long, narrow gallery, with closed doors on each side ; then an end room, with a pleasant window looking over open spaces, and the sun shining in.

An elderly woman, in the gray gown, with knotted girdle, the white linen cap and bands, and a large rosary at her side, sat in a plain wooden armchair, made more comfortable at the back with a folded gray blanket.

" Approach, my child. It is that I have rheumatism. Seat yourself here." And she motioned to a chair placed beside her.

Cyrilla came near with a courteous movement of salutation. But she delayed nothing for any possible peculiar etiquette of the place, or any strangeness of the circumstances. She went straight to her errand.

" I am here," she said, "to make inquiry about some one — Mrs. Raye — who has been ill here."

" It was not the name she called herself when she first arrived. But that matters not. We found it, afterwards, among some things. She died ; she was penitent ; she received the consolation of the church ; she expected some one."

" She expected me."

" If not, the little box was to be sent. I have guarded it." Mother Marthe laid her finger upon a small bell beside her, on the table. Rill reached forward her own hand.

" If you please — wait ! Of what did she repent ? "

" My child, it was of all her life ! "

Rill grew paler and paler. " What was all her life ? " she demanded. " I must know."

" Poor little one ! but it is that which you cannot know. Indeed, it was the life of the blessed Saint Mary Magdalene, before she came to the Christ ! "

" *My mother !* "

The brief sentences before had been in French. These two words broke forth in Rill's own tongue. She covered her face. The good Mother leaned toward her, and laid a kind hand on her head. She spoke to her with gentle, religious words. " It is absolved. We pray for her. Solace yourself. The Holy Magdalene takes part with her. They are together at the feet of Christ."

" I never knew it; all these years ! It was a wickedness."

"It was God's will. You were not meant to know ; you have been kept safe."

"*Safe !* — And why have I been '*meant to know*' — too late !" Her words were bitter.

"That also is God's will. It is for cause of some other thing in your life, perhaps, that you do not know yet, even. Nothing is too late." The Mother touched her bell. The Sister who had led Rill hither, entered.

"The little box," said Mother Marthe.

It was a shabby, old-fashioned thing, of pasteboard and painted velvet. Inside were a few trinkets : a chain of coral, a mosaic pin, with — the pity ! — a white lily for design ; a wedding ring ; a creased, worn paper folded into a small square, the name "Rill" written upon it in ink faded to a rusty faintness. Cyrilla opened it, as one forced. It held a round, soft, yellow lock of a child's hair. She had kept that, all through ! The ring was marked inside — "M. R. to E. B." There was a date of twenty years before.

Cyrilla laid all back, silently. There was no doubt, now. She stood up, with the queer little box in her hand. "I must go," she said. "There is nothing to do here. I must get — back." She could not say "home." I must find out where home is to be," she thought, vaguely.

"I ought to thank you," she roused to say. "I

owe you very much. I will write to you. I will
send something for your House of Hope. Good-
by!"

The Mother looked at her wistfully; murmured
some invocation of blessing, but perceived no more
that she could do; and Rill, moving mechanically,
followed the silent Sister who waited to lead her
out. She got to the street again, as one walking
with dull effort in a dream; reëntered the carriage,
and was driven back to the St. James.

She found her way in, and up to her room,
alone; no obsequious attention met her; but presently a clerk came to her door, and asked her when
she expected the friends who were to arrive, and
what rooms they would require.

"I expect no friends."

The two looked at each other in mutual surprise.

"I shall take the afternoon train for Boston."

The man bowed slightly, and went away. In a
moment a maid came and asked her, with scant
deference, if she would mind having her trunk
taken down to another room, since she was to leave
directly. This would be wanted, if she pleased.

She was put into a dim little one-windowed
place, opening upon the court. She went to the
dining-room at the lunch hour, and tried to eat, for
she felt faint and ill. Then she had to wait two
hours and a half alone, in the dim little room.

At half past four she was at the station. She
put herself on board the train, and found her
number in the sleeping-car. She begged the porter
to make up her berth as soon as possible ; but for
some time longer the seats were needed, and it was
eight o'clock before she could lie down to rest.
A thick, soft snow had been falling for two hours,
but she did not know of that.

Meanwhile, another Boston telegram had been
received at the St. James, and the spacious, cheerful corner room, and one adjoining, *en suite*, were
being prepared in reserve for Mrs. and Miss Rextell, to arrive to-night.

CHAPTER XXVIII.

NUMBER ——TY-TWO MOUNT VERNON STREET.

CYRILLA could not sleep. The best she could do
was to hold herself outwardly still, and let the
night go over her. The car was full. She lay and
thought how strange the isolation of human creatures is.

Here were some twoscore souls, in close community and limit; in their present circumstance
the same, yet utterly disintegrant; knowing, asking, caring nothing of each other's lives; certain
to fly apart on divergent lines the moment their
common point was reached. Would it be like that
in the Kingdom of Heaven? Would nobody in
that multitude ask how it fared with any other, or
seek to touch a sympathy, or render a help? Humanity was a queer thing. If it were not for small
personal link and place, it would be a huge in-
sanity.

And where, now, were her own link and place?

She had had so little to hold by; yet, by that
little, she had seemed to be a part of something

larger ; she had neighborhood and a life. Now, she had broken away from all. She had not aunt Amelia ; she could not have her any more. How could she forgive her for that other life cast adrift and never searched for ? For the robbing of it, that had been the taking and keeping of herself, in ignorance ? She belonged to no one. The unreal past was swept away. With it had gone a beautiful half dream of a future. She could not look at that. She hid the eyes of her thought, and thrust it from her.

She must go somewhere when she reached Boston. Where, and with what account of herself ? She was a detached particle. She had no relation with the world. She was an atom against a universe.

Her head ached, her thoughts grew wandering. Was she going to be ill ?

The train stopped. At some station, of course. It would go on in a minute. But a great many minutes went by, and she began to wonder. There were quick footsteps through the car ; a lantern flashed back and forth. She parted her curtains and looked out. Other faces were looking out also.

" Halloo ! What 's this ? " a man asked of a brakeman, who hurried through.

" Breakdown, just ahead. Freight train. Engine and three cars half way down to the river, in the mud."

" Where are we ? " somebody else took up the inquiry, further on.

"Two or three miles from White River Junction." And the door at the farther end slammed a period to the words.

Rill reached her watch out into the light. The hands pointed to half past one. She lay back and tried to be quiet. There were voices and confused movements for a while, a busy passing to and fro outside ; then it grew still. The trouble and the work were far ahead ; here, there was nothing to do but wait. Waiting and listening, she fell into a half sleep, and hours went by.

The dull gray morning came, and found them there. Five hours lost. They crept slowly toward White River Junction at just the time when they were scheduled due at their journey's end.

Rill had eaten nothing since her slight lunch the day before. She had one orange and two or three little biscuits in her bag. People were asking and answering questions about the probable start, and concerning breakfast. Everything was in confusion ; tracks crowded ; they stopped far outside the station. Trains up and down were blocked ; theirs must wait for the regular morning express from St. Albans, and go down with that. Breakfast might be had at a farmhouse up yonder hill. The snow was falling fast; it was many inches deep already. Rill followed a party of the passengers from the car, and out upon the track side. If she could only go and get something hot. She was faint for food, and her throat was dry and aching. But her feet began to be damp directly, and it was a long way up the untrodden hill. Some men came back who had been to the farmhouse. "Not much of anything there," she heard them say. "Pretty hard truck, what there is of it." She turned back and climbed into the car. The berths were folded away, and the seats arranged. She must rest as best she could, and it was so hard to sit up! She ate her orange, but the biscuits were dry and irritating. How long would it be, and how should she hold out?

"St. Albans train due here at twelve. We'll get to Boston at half past six, if we have all the luck there's left." That was what some one said presently, who came in behind her. Rill leaned back her head and shut her eyes. The tears filled their lids. "You poor thing!" she said to herself, pityingly. "No one knows; and for *that* reason you have *got* to keep up!" So she instantly rebuked and compelled herself.

She held out in her determination not to go back to Wewachet. Indeed, she would scarcely be able to do so now, upon her late arrival. What then? A hotel? She recoiled from the idea; she had experienced enough in that sort. And if she should be unable, once in bed, to be up again to-morrow! Would they let her have a room at the Christian Association? She thought so; that was what it was for, a resource in such emergencies. Yet, again, if she should be ill? And truly she was ill enough already.

She gave up, at last, on one point. She went into the telegraph office before they left White River, and sent a message to Miss Haven. "On my way to Boston. Train delayed. Arrive 6.30. Please meet and advise me."

Miss Haven was in town; Mr. King was not. Miss Haven would see her safe; afterward she could think what to do.

Miss Haven had had an earlier dispatch. The wires had been lively along the line. While Rill grew more and more ill and troubled as the train made its slow, hindered progress, all order unhinged, stations blocked with waiting cars, engines snorting on all the sidings, reckoning changing hour by hour — the august Melcombe had been up and down between the railroad offices and Beacon Hill, watching and reporting the successive delays of belated No. 50.

When at last, at half past ten, poor Rill mustered her remaining strength to pick up shawl and bag, and stumble forth upon the platform of the Pullman, half blinded by a weak dizziness — bewildered with rush and stun — she distinguished nothing ; she only kept fast hold of one intention and rehearsed order — " To the Christian Association ; " and when kind arms were put about her, and some deferent hand took wrap and satchel from her, she saw nothing of the gray-haired, distinguished serving-man, and barely recognized Miss Haven's tender voice. " Will you take me to the Young Women's Christian Association ? " was all she said.

" Poor child ! of course I will. I 'll see you safe."

And the dear, prevaricating woman, as she almost lifted Rill into the carriage, said exoneratively in her own mind, " Christian Association ! Wherever else there may be one in Boston, I know there 's one at number ——ty-two Mount Vernon Street ! "

CHAPTER XXIX.

LIFE IS NEVER OVER.

MRS. REXTELL and Margaret returned the next day. A fresh illustration of the difficult problems of hotel keeping had enlarged the already wide experience of the clerk of the St. James. Mrs. Rextell had made her first inquiry as she was being ushered to the corner room, and had sent down instant word that the heavy trunks need not be brought upstairs. "Since Miss Raye is not here, we shall leave in the morning," she said.

And a few minutes after, she had rung her bell and dispatched the telegram which Miss Haven had received at breakfast.

The next afternoon, without having seen Cyrilla, Miss Bonable went home. "I 'm neither nurse nor patient," she said. "I have n't the privilege of the sick-room, and I can't stay here, outside."

"Dear Miss Bonable, she could n't bear it now. But it will all come right." So Miss Haven took her down to the train and bade her good-by.

Miss Bonable said her own sentence over in her

mind, as Rill had conned to herself against her bewilderment that inquiry for the Christian Association. "She's with the Rextells in Boston. They've all been off on some sort of a jaunt. I stopped with Miss Haven while they were away."

She said it to half a dozen people before she got to Wewachet and Brook Lane ; and nothing but that, or some slight variation of its wording, could be gotten out of her. When one or two adventurously pushed the inquiry " Where ? " she answered them, " Oh. I don't know ; up country somewhere, to see the snow ; " and then nipped her own arm secretly. inside her muff, or trod vindictively upon one tender foot with the boot-heel of her other, for the evasion.

At the cottage, Clementhy Pond opened the door.

" She's in Boston — with the Rextells. They've been off — I stopped with Miss Haven — she'll be back, — there, let me go upstairs ! "

The day following was Sunday. Miss Amelia went to church. She put on her handsome new winter suit that Cyrilla and Miss Haven had persuaded her into buying. They had persuaded her into several things of late.

People said Miss Bonable had grown handsome since her illness. She had been growing handsome — as such women do who are not beauties in their youth, but who have the soul of beauty in them —

for twenty years, only she would never let it appear. To-day, she would show a brave outside; nobody should guess her trouble, or the anxious pain with which she waited, while she faced the wondering little worshiping world of Wewachet in her sealskin cloak and her brown plush bonnet with the cluster of poppy-buds above the brim, and her soft hair, that yet matched the plush and seal where the light bronzed them, gently crimped below. The hair was parted — she despised a bang — but it lay in softening waves and little escaping curly tips about her brow. " I 'll *act* easy-minded," she said, "at any rate."

So she met her acquaintances in the porch and aisle, and on the street, and said her say as the minister had said his text; a thing chosen beforehand. I am afraid she forgot the text while she remembered her own lesson, and rung the little changes on it after she had heard the sermon.

At home again, Clementhy met her with a note, and a bunch of roses. A man had brought them from the Rextell place, she said. The note had been sent from Boston, soon after breakfast.

" We think Cyrilla in no present danger, but she needs entire quiet and great care. You shall know from day to day. Trust me with her for a little while; try to be patient. You have borne so much; bear yet a little more; it must all come right.   E. P. H."

"And there's a gentleman in the parlor; he called Friday. I did n't tell you sooner, for I kind o' thought you might as well have one thing to a time," said Clementhy Pond.

The two women had come into the little sitting-room. Clementhy had lighted the laid fire in the north parlor fireplace, and shut the door upon the visitor there. Miss Bonable would be back "immejutly after church," she had told him.

Clementhy retired to her kitchen, and to the plump chicken she was basting so delicately brown for dinner. Amelia Bonable crossed the hall and opened the parlor door. She had the roses, tea-pink and buff and creamy-white, in her hands.

A tall, broad, fine-countenanced man, in unexceptional dress worn with an accustomed ease, stood facing her. Deep, handsome, hazel - gray eyes looked out upon her from under brows bent level with an habitually keen, perceptive intelligence. Two strong hands were reached forward to her, as their owner made two quick, decisive steps to meet her. The roses all fell, sweet and scattered, on the floor.

" Amy ! "

" Mark ! "

So, after the sixteen years, they met again. With a great flood of color rushing over her face and sweeping swiftly back, she clung to the grasp

of his hands, and cried out, — her voice sharp with
sudden release of pain, her lesson still struggling,
mechanically, with more spontaneous words, —
"Oh, Mark! She is in Boston. She's been away.
A little jaunt" — she laughed with a tearful
catch, and the truth broke forth. "Mark! Mark!
She's been — alone — to Canada! Loraine wrote
to her. She's come back sick, and I can't be with
her. She won't forgive me, for she don't know!
And I was hard with her, for I was so afraid!"

"Loraine!" ejaculated the man, with a stern
emphasis, seizing but one point in the interjected
statement.

"Loraine is dead." She said that slowly. He
had let go her hands.

A great light rose up strangely in Mark Raye's
face. It was not a flash, a joy, an exultation; it
was a solemn sunrise. He did not say a word;
but his eyes looked down, with that deep glow
in them, and sought Amelia's. She lifted hers,
softly; they were young and sweet, as they filled
with the shining that came from his. He did not
touch her; he did not speak; they stood quiet and
awed, as under some supreme announcement and
benediction.

Then, presently, he stooped down at her feet.
"You have dropped all your roses;" and saying
that, began to gather them together. She waited

till he stood up and put them in her hands. "I wish I could do that with all that has dropped out of your life," he said.

"Oh, Mark!" she answered, "I have been wicked. I have felt as if I were somebody that had died. I have talked about 'when I was alive.' And life is never over!"

"Never more than just begun, Amy!"

Nothing plainer than that was said; but angels' speech could not be plainer.

They ate their Sunday dinner together; and Clementhy went about serving them in a kind of homely rapture that came of an instinct of some wonderful, heavenly thing, she knew not what. "It was like carrying round the Sacrament!" she said to herself in the kitchen while she washed the dishes.

Afterward, they talked much of Cyrilla. "If she will only get well, and understand, and forgive me," Amelia said.

"She will have to forgive you. She will have to forgive us both together."

"I have watched her, and kept her down; I was looking out always for the Braitway in her; and all the time she has been clear Raye!"

CHAPTER XXX.

It was many days before Cyrilla could be allowed to enter into details on her own part, or receive any detailed information, such as Miss Haven was reserving only for the first right moment, or such as present events were making ready for her hearing.

Even in Wewachet it had not become known that Miss Bonable had been visited by a strange guest; far less had any idea drifted into its atmosphere that there was on the earth any one who might appear there with such surprise and significance. Mr. Raye had a few days' business in New York; and had wisely gone away to do it.

It had been hard to persuade Cyrilla to rest easy in the kind keeping of the Rextells. In those first hours, she had told Miss Haven, with bitter pain, the bare facts, which Miss Bonable had thus had it in her power to announce to Marcus Raye; then, with only the often-urged entreaty to be put somewhere, to have a place found for her where she could with a clear right stay, and the protest that she belonged to nobody now, and could let nobody be mixed up with her any more, she relapsed into a kind of passive reticence, and lay hour after hour in a mere weakness and forced endurance. Miss Bonable's name agitated her dangerously. "She meant right by me, and I ought to remember it. But she did wrong — wrong! How *could* she give her sister up!"

"Perhaps there are things in the whole story that you do not know; what you have to do now is to get strong, and to let us help you. Then the meaning of all this, and your own part and duty, may appear."

Miss Haven spoke with a grave, tender authority. It reminded Rill of Mother Marthe's word, "Because of some other thing in your life that you do not know of yet, perhaps, this has been let come to you so late." It was all a distressful puzzle; she could see nothing clear; she had not light enough to believe by.

Yet her strong, young physical powers asserted themselves; in ten days she was able to be up; and then Mrs. Rextell said, "We will all go to Wewachet and keep Christmas. After that, we will make plans."

Mrs. Rextell always carried all her own way. Even if one meant finally to contradict her, one

had to be swept a little distance first by the current of her vigorous, kindly intent. Cyrilla had
at last yielded herself as one simply befriended in
a need, to the care given to her illness ; inwardly,
she set herself in a stern new attitude to these
friends who had become so dear. She could not
be of them any more, — she, the daughter of a Mag-
dalen. It was even in this very spirit of utter
humbling that she accepted kindness from them as
pure favor, for a while. She confessed herself an
object of the gentle charity that sought out such
and benefited them. But she meant to be very
proud — to loneliness — in her own way, by and
by !

Rill absolutely resisted the Wewachet plan at
first. " I am able to go somewhere else," she said.
" I do not belong with you."

Miss Haven passed that over. She only asked
her, " What level, then, do you propose to seek ? "
and to that, Rill could say nothing.

" But how can I go so near Miss Bonable, not
meaning to go home to her ? I do not wish " —

" To hurt, or to insult her. No, indeed. Rill,
I can but assure you of one thing. If you do not
let yourself be guided in this, you will find that
you ought to have done so. You are in a dark
place. Give me your hand, and I will lead you
out. I will show you where you are, which is what

you do not know.   But your eyes will not bear all
the light at once.   Believe me."

Rill misunderstood her strangely.   She remembered that other word, " Believe in me, as I believe
in you."   For fear of the very betrayal that resistance would be, she reserved her protest.   It did not
matter much.   If she could not escape, she could
face and settle the crises of her unhappy circumstance.   In all their talks, no word had been
spoken of Putnam King.   He was away, upon
those professional errands; he had been out to
Duluth, and down to St. Louis, across to Washington, back to Boston, and away to Washington
again with Mr. Arbicon.   In the midst of his work
he found unwonted time to write to aunt Elizabeth,
tell her of his doings, and ask the news of Wewachet.   How much or how little, therefore, he might
know of befallings there, rested with the golden
gossip; and she assumed it to be quite her own
business.

They went out to " The Cedars."   It was a mile
away from Wewachet village, and half as far, in
another direction, from Brook Lane.   Perhaps nobody need know.

The large low house was warmed and lighted.
One beautiful mullioned window shone with amber
and crimson panes, like a flash of jewels.

Mrs. Jollis met them, smiling, at the door.

"Miss Raye is tired," Mrs. Rextell said. "We will go right upstairs, and you may send tea to my dressing-room."

Resist as she might, endure as she must, Rill could but feel the graciousness of such home bringing, such putting of her in the carefully considered place. After the tea, she was shown quietly to her sleeping chamber. Mrs. Rextell kissed her at the door. "I will leave you by yourself, dear child," she said. "But Agnes shall look in by and by, to see if you need anything."

How patient they were with her, in her withdrawn, renouncing mood! She turned, and went into the softly lighted apartment. It was the pond lily room.

No word that could have been spoken would have said it to her like that. "It is where I put my very dearest, sweetest young girl friends."

And all about her, plainly manifest, shone even fairer sign and message, which she could not ignore or refuse. In the " beauty of the lilies " it was hieroglyphed; no matter from what dark ooze the stems might spring; they, blooming into the sun, looked up pure white. Rill took the blessed comforting for more than herself; was it not the possible soul-blossoming of penitence ? None the less, the lily carries up its memory into the sun; it is chained beneath the waters; it must abide in a meek solitude; it can only lift itself and breathe its sweetness into Heaven.

The next morning Rill and Miss Haven sat together. "Dear Miss Haven," said Rill, "how long before you mean to lead me out, and show me the way? I cannot stay here, in the House Beautiful, you know." She spoke gently, and with the shadow of a smile; yet with the same resolute placing of herself in her new attitude, of one on a separate, different, practical plane.

"Dear Rill, how long do you mean to hold out against Miss Bonable?"

"It is not a question of holding out. I cannot help it that I have no place with her." The sternness had come over the young face again.

"Rill! If you let this thing harden in your heart, you will grow harder than ever she did. For in her hardness there has been no resentment."

"Perhaps I may. That, too, may be a part of my inheritance — with the cause for the resentment added." She spoke with a deliberate coldness.

"Cyrilla! This must be broken up! I must tell you. You are strong enough to bear it now. You can inherit *nothing* from Miss Bonable. You have no right even to her faults. You never had a claim upon her. Her love — everything she has given you — has been free gift."

" I know I had no claim. I did not belong to
her. I belonged to my father and my mother.
She was only my aunt."

" She was only your father's first wife's sister.
Your mother was no kin to her at all."

" Miss Haven!" Every bit of color had gone
out of Cyrilla's face.

" She never wanted you to know."

Cyrilla had leaned forward while Miss Haven
had been speaking, her hands clasped tightly across
her knees; her expression had grown fixed, intent.
Now it seemed as if she were hypnotized in the
attitude. She remained motionless, breathless, for
a minute or more. The minute felt long to them
both. Then a gentle wave of color returned to the
pale face; the eyes lighted and softened with an
expression that gave itself instantly to a remembrance of great kindness; and the hands reached
out humbly to Miss Haven, as Cyrilla stood up, a
certain hard-used dignity retained in her erectness.
" You are *very* good. I am glad I know *something*,
at last. It was time. I must go away, and think,"
she said.

" Think as your thoughts are led, dear child,"
Miss Haven answered her; and Rill passed on into
the pond lily room.

There it came over her, with its full significance
and bearing; with the new doubt and question also.

Where were her proud protest and resentment,
in which she had been so strong? Where was
her great injury, that she was never to forgive?
Where was her independence, even, in which she
could break loose old bonds and go away into such
new life as she should choose?

"She has cared for me all these years, and I was
nothing to her!" Her honest heart said this, and
shamed her. "Am I even sure that all my — all
the other — said, was true? *This* was falsified;
why not that? Is there any one else on all the
earth to whom I do belong? Is there any likeli-
hood that I can claim, or take, the least thing that
way? If there were anything, is it not all due to
her, — Miss Bonable? Am I not due, myself, to
her? And yet, if I am helpless now, how, for that
very reason, can I go back?" It was all a seethe
of torturing perplexity.

But at last it came to her, — the one plain, first
step. "I must go and ask her to forgive me — I
who thought I could not forgive her — and I must
own my great debt to her, and thank her — as if
any thanking could go back, and take all up, and
make acknowledgement! And then I may go
away, and earn my bread."

She came back into Miss Haven's room; she
had put on her cloak and bonnet, and her warm
furs. The weight of the clothing oppressed her;

she was yet so weak. She caught her breath shortly, and a strange, trembling fatigue came into her limbs.

Miss Haven looked up with an exclamation: " Rill ! What can you possibly mean to do ? "

" I mean to go to the cottage. I mean to go down on my knees to Miss Bonable, and beg her pardon. Then — I don't know yet what I mean to do."

" But you cannot walk. Mrs. Rextell — Margaret — we might have the carriage. I will take you."

" I will not go in anybody's carriage. I will not be taken. I will get there, somehow." Even as she spoke she dropped into a chair. " I shall be all right presently," she said. " Or — perhaps — if they would send for Oates ; I would go in the depot carriage ; may be I must do that."

" Now, Rill, you are acting hastily ; you are in an extreme again. You must let us judge for you, and help you. Let me go with you ; you are unfit to be alone."

" I am not fit " — burst from Rill's lips; and then the lips quivered, and she gathered back her willful resolution against absolute break-down. " If you will come with me in Oates's carriage — to the end of the lane — and let me go in alone from there," she said. So Oates was telephoned for.

" You are quite right to go ; and you shall go as you please," Mrs. Rextell said. " And you shall come back — or you shall stay there — as you please, then." The very slight emphasis upon the alternative marked confidence in Cyrilla's complete reparation, and its natural method.

Cyrilla only said, gravely, " I have no right there."

CHAPTER XXXI.

"MOTHER."

"You will not come again, Mark, till Cyrilla knows. It would not be fair." That was what Amy Bonable had said to Marcus Raye at the end of his first visit.

"I will come when you send for me. I shall be at Young's Hotel. How soon will you tell her?"

"As soon as I can see her. If she does not come here I shall go to her."

And that was the way it happened that when Cyrilla left Miss Haven in the carriage at the entrance to Brook Lane, and began with slow, difficult steps the walk toward Miss Bonable's door, that person herself came at a brisk, determined pace around the winding turn across the little bridge, and met the prodigal.

"Child!"

"Miss Bonable!"

"Don't say a word, here in the street! You are perfectly white. You are n't fit to be out. Oh, Rill! There, hush up; come back — home!"

and a strong arm was reached out, and a hand
grasped Rill's arm to help and lift her, and then
would not stop there, but by sudden impulse put itself around the girl, and Rill was drawn close to the
warm support of aunt Amelia's furred shoulder.

Miss Haven ordered her driver on to Crooke
Corner.

Within the cottage, a bright pine-wood fire
burned in the sitting-room. Miss Bonable pulled
a cushioned chair to the hearth and set Rill in it.
"You're not to say a word till you've had a
tumbler of hot wine whey. And then — I've got
to talk to you."

To make sure of her purpose, Miss Bonable
whisked from the room, and went to prepare the
wine whey herself. But when she came back,
Rill was on a low hassock at the chair-foot. She
put back the glass with a gentle, imploring motion.

"Sit here, please; and let me speak first. I
could not swallow unless I did. I have been so
wrong. I have been so ignorant. I am so ashamed
and sorry. I have come to tell you so. I want
you to forgive me, and do what you like with me.
Only I wish I could pay back something of all I
owe. I would like to be your servant."

What became of the glass of whey for the moment, I am not sure; I think Miss Bonable set it
down on the hearth. She seated herself upon the

rug before Rill, a little lower yet than the low cushion. "Rill, I want you to forgive me," she said. "You don't quite know all what for. I was going to you to tell you. You must forgive everybody. We must begin again. Things are all broken up; a whole piece of my life has dropped right out, and there is nothing left of it but you. You must stay; the rest of it is cast into the sea."

Her eyes were lifted up to Rill's; they were large and dark — and soft — as Rill had never seen them before; the tears were brimming them.

"Dear — how young you look! How sweet you are!" cried Rill, gazing at the miracle of the woman gone back across that hard, abolished piece of her life to the lovely time and self that had been before. Rill had paused for a name, before she could speak at all; then that "dear" came and uttered itself. The two put their arms about each other's neck, and kissed each other.

There is nothing so tender as repentance. To be forgiven is to love; more than with no need of repentance. That is why God lets wrong and mistake be possible to us; that this most blessed thing may be possible also.

After that, the long story of explanation could wait a little. Somehow, they both knew, and it was scarcely needed. Miss Bonable made Cyrilla drink the wine whey.

"Now, can you bear to hear a new, strange thing? It is what I have got to tell you, before it comes and tells itself. Cyrilla, your father has come back. He is waiting to know that he can see you. He will be here to-night."

Cyrilla looked in the sweet, changed face, and divined what had so transfigured it. It was a human heart that had come to its own again; as out of age and pain and separation hearts enter paradise.

When Miss Haven came back from Crooke Corner and stopped at the cottage, Miss Bonable met her at the door. "Will you send this down to the noon mail, *sure?* It is all right," she said. And again Miss Haven drove away.

Cyrilla was sent up to her own little east room to sleep and rest. The afternoon wore quietly away; the early sunset came, and the east room was dim, with only reflected lights. But far over toward the new sunrising that would be to-morrow, was the rosy glow in which to-day went down.

In the twilight she arose and ordered her dress and her hair. How strange it was to be going down to — aunt Amelia? What name should she call Miss Bonable by, now? It must be a name of love, and not of cold constraint; but it could not be — she did not wish it to be — the name she had known her by through all their misknowing.

While she stood and thought of this, she heard the door open, and the firm entering tread of a man.

There were low voices down beneath, in the little sitting-room. She could hear the fresh fire crackle in the chimney. Her father was there; she must go to him — to them.

Slowly she passed down the stairway. It was not a thing to hurry to, eagerly; it was a strange, solemn meeting and making known; when she opened the door, the two figures stood there by the hearth, waiting. Both turned; the man's hands were held out. "Are you my little daughter?" he said.

Cyrilla came up with a shy womanly dignity in her face; she had been deprived of her "little-daughter"-hood; she could not go right back into that. "I suppose so," she said, pathetically, putting her own hands in his. "But oh, I ought to have known you all these years!"

"You must forgive us both. We thought of you. It seemed the best. There were many things that could not be quite explained; there were things to guard you from."

"I know. And I have been hard to guard. But, indeed, I was not so much to be — afraid of."

"That was my mistake," said Miss Bonable. "And I am sorry. But you shall know everything now that you have a right to."

"I do know. And I think we will put it all away."

Marcus Raye looked at the girl as she spoke, with a wondering pleasure in his heart, at her sweet, frank nobleness. "You are like my mother, Rill," he said.

"But you don't know all. And it should not be kept back a minute longer. Mark, tell her." Miss Bonable came to Marcus Raye's side as she spoke, and put one hand in his, while she laid the other on Cyrilla's shoulder.

Cyrilla lifted her eyes quickly, and flashed a look at each as they stood there. "It does n't need telling," she said. "It is good. I am glad, I am glad" — and her voice took a tender, happy ring in it — "that I shall have a real, true name to call you by, — *Mother!*"

In that instant she gave all. Miss Bonable let go the father's hand, and folded her arms about the daughter, and held her close.

"Will you go to the other side of the world with us, Rill?" asked Mr. Raye, a minute later.

"I will go with you, if it is beyond the world!"

CHAPTER XXXII.

THE coming home of a rich Australian father to
a girl who had not been supposed to have any father at all, was a great windfall to Wewachet. It
was much more than a windfall; it was the dropping into their midst of a wonderful, magnificent
aerolite. They gathered round the great phenome-
non with all their little hammers. They tried to
chip it here and there; to get off crumbs and corners, that should seem to multiply its contents and
significance. But they did not get at the heart of
it, with all their tapping; until Miss Haven was
duly authorized to disclose it in such a way as she
pleased.

Connie Norris came over, one day, to Crooke
Corner. She had something on her mind. She had
promised George Craigan to give him a clear,
final answer that evening. Somehow, she felt as
if Miss Haven could help her; could counsel her,
or give her light. Miss Haven held the threads of
things in Wewachet. Perhaps she could say some-

thing to her, even indirectly, which would settle
her mind upon contingent and still anxious points.

She found Dr. Harriman there. Would this
help or hinder? She began to think how she
could approach her matter without a too plain
speaking. It was a chance, undoubtedly. Over
Miss Haven's shoulder she could hint a need, a
worry, that might make oblique appeal to Dr.
Harriman.

But Miss Haven had her news to tell. She had
already given it to the doctor. "Do you know
there is an engagement out?" she asked Cornelia.

"No, — where?" responded Connie, quickly;
the mistrust striking her that her own decision
might, Wewachet-fashion, have been forestalled.
She did not pause to consider that it would not
have been Miss Haven's fashion to force the acknowledgment in this way.

"In Brook Lane," said Miss Haven, smiling;
and Connie saw what she thought a conscious answering smile upon Dr. Harriman's face. She did
not consider the fashion of this announcement,
either. Nothing is inconsistent to an intense pre-
possession.

"I am sure," she said hastily, "I hope everybody will be very happy. I ought to hope so, for
I am in the category myself. I came to tell you"
— the sudden adaptation of her errand slipped into

a fib — "I am going to be married to Mr. George Craigan."

Instantly they both shook hands with her, offering hearty congratulations. Her little victory was over. The defeat remained.

"But I have not told you," said Miss Haven, when they had given due time and words to the interpolated tidings. "You will like to know. It is a beautiful old story. It is Mr. Raye who is to marry Miss Bonable. They cared for each other a great while ago, but it was given up. Rill is very happy."

Connie did her best; she was as much astonished as she need be; the quality of her astonishment was only fully known to herself.

She had committed herself. That evening she gave her answer to George Craigan. She took her satisfactions, such as they were, as such brides do.

"I mean to be married in church," she told Sue Wilder. "It's a great deal better fun. And I'm going to Washington. I shall see Mrs. Cleveland. You know they say I look like her. Mr. Craigan is going to build for us. And, oh, Sue! I mean to have such a lovely morning-room!"

"I hope you find Mr. George Craigan of use to you in your plans," said Sue, with sudden sarcasm.

Connie stared. "What *do* you mean?" she

cried. She understood the allusion well enough, but she could not comprehend it from Sue Wilder.

Sue was simply disenchanted and indignant. She had put heart and faith in her friend's other romance. She had thought George Craigan was the "obstacle." She had meekly admired and idealized as she was bid. Now this was too much.

There was something to be and to come, both in and for Sue Wilder, better than following in the wake of Connie Norris's fantasies and flirtations.

"Sue has grown into Susan," Rill said of her afterward, upon an occasion. "And Susan is sweet and sober, and strong and womanly."

It was long afterward, when much in circumstance and event had taken fixed and accepted place. She said it to Dr. Harriman, the strength of whose finer character had asserted itself in the rare achievement of gradually replacing a disappointed selfishness of love with a high generosity of friendship.

Rill Raye had revealed him to himself. She had given him better than her love. The magnanimity in him, that she had compelled by her confident demand, discovered itself to him as a capacity from which it was a gladness to act, whatever, like the swift athletes of old, he might have to cast away in the noble urgency of pressing onward to his higher mark.

The reader may, if she pleases, construct a possible side sequel from this influence and bearing, which my story has not space for. I will neither affirm nor overthrow her conclusion. It shall be as she likes best.

Miss Haven began to think she had undertaken a good deal. Now, she had Putnam King upon her hands. She wrote to him every word of what had happened. Of course, Putnam came, at the earliest practicable moment, to Wewachet.

"It is not possible she will do that!" he exclaimed, when aunt Elizabeth told him of the plan of going to Adelaide. For the moment, he almost believed that he had believed in a delusion.

"I told you she would burn and drown, in her own heart, for those she cared for. It is high sacrifice. So high, that it is glad. It is for you, as much as for them. If she thinks of anything else, she believes that it would wrong you."

"There is simply but one thing to be done, and I shall go straight and do it."

"Go to her father, then; it is your only chance."

CHAPTER XXXIII.

" OUGHT I ? "

"You ask a great deal of me," said Marcus Raye. "But I will tell her. I will even urge the cause. It will need urging, for her scruples of right, and her sense of present duty, will be strong. I have known Rill but a little while, but I know her well enough to be sure that the more her own wish pleads for you, the more she will refuse."

" I must leave it with you — now," said Putnam King. "But I shall not leave it with you finally. I shall speak for myself."

" Very good," said Marcus Raye. " I can even hope you may succeed." And he gave the young man a well-pleased smile, and a hearty grasp of the hand.

" We shall have to give her up," the father said to his promised wife. " We shall have to do more ; we must even push her out of the new nest."

Rill said her determined nay, at the first word. It was so determined, that it was easy to see it was against herself.

"You have no right, if you care for him. If you have entered into his life, you belong there, and must stay."

"But, father, — even if all the rest were right and easy, how could I? It is hard to say it to you, — but I am *her* child. Ought I to hold myself "— she could not utter the rest.

Then Marcus Raye spoke out of the depth of his full-grown, manly nature. "You are the child of humanity. Its possibilities are all in you. They have come through many channels. No one can trace all his own antecedents. She — when she was your mother — with whatever faults, was at her brightest and sweetest. She was gay and loving. You are like her in that. You are born of the best of her. Her sin was weakness; you are strong. Live for your mother, Rill; live out the other nature of her, from which she took the mistaken turn. She is turned back to it now, we will believe. And you are *my* child, Rill; and so, my mother's, who was the grandest woman I ever knew."

.   .   .   .

"No one but my father could have persuaded me. No, not you, Putnam. I should have resisted you for the love of you. Nothing could have assured me but being his child. If he had not come home, *nothing* would have been mended."

And nobody knew the hand the Golden Gossip had had in that.

Beautiful upon the hard places of the earth are the feet of one who bringeth *good* tidings; who *publisheth peace.*

www.ingramcontent.com/pod-product-compliance
Lightning Source LLC
Chambersburg PA
CBHW021111270326
41929CB00009B/828